Extraordinary Old Dogs

Laura Greaves is a multi-award-winning journalist, author and proud 'crazy dog lady'. She has spent more than twenty years writing for newspapers and magazines in Australia and around the world and is the former editor of *Dogs Life* magazine. She is the author of the collections *Incredible Dog Journeys*, *Dogs with Jobs*, *The Rescuers* and *Miracle Mutts*, the children's book *Amazing Dogs with Amazing Jobs*, as well as three romantic comedy novels, *Be My Baby*, *The Ex-Factor* and *Two Weeks 'Til Christmas*, all of which feature an extensive supporting cast of cheeky canines. She has twice won the Dog Writers Association of America's Rio Award, which recognises the best book about a dog that has impacted a human's life in a profoundly positive way.

Also by Laura Greaves

Incredible Dog Journeys
Dogs with Jobs
The Rescuers
Amazing Dogs with Amazing Jobs
Miracle Mutts

Extraordinary Old Dogs

Laura Greaves

Uplifting True Tales of
Remarkable Seniors

MICHAEL JOSEPH
an imprint of
PENGUIN BOOKS

MICHAEL JOSEPH

UK | USA | Canada | Ireland | Australia
India | New Zealand | South Africa | China

Michael Joseph is part of the Penguin Random House group of companies,
whose addresses can be found at global.penguinrandomhouse.com.

Penguin
Random House
Australia

First published by Michael Joseph, 2020
Text copyright © Laura Greaves, 2020

Cover design by James Rendall © Penguin Random House Australia Pty Ltd
Cover photograph courtesy Paula Puncher/EyeEm/Getty Images
Typeset in Sabon by Midland Typesetters, Australia
Printed and bound in Australia by Griffin Press, an accredited ISO AS/NZS 14001
Environmental Management Systems printer.

A catalogue record for this
book is available from the
National Library of Australia

ISBN: 978 1 76089 477 1

penguin.com.au

MIX
Paper from
responsible sources
FSC® C009448

This book is dedicated to the memory of my two spectacular grandmothers, Peggy Weaver (1928–2009) and Julie Earl (1930–2020), the first women in my life to show me that age is just a number.

*Blessed is the person who has
earned the love of an old dog*
— Sidney Jeanne Seward

Contents

Introduction

This book was inspired by my ancient puppy, Tex. (All dogs are puppies, by the way, regardless of age or size. Irish wolfhound the size of a horse? Puppy. Sixteen-year-old cattle dog? Also a puppy.)

At the time of writing, Tex, a Nova Scotia Duck Tolling Retriever, is three months away from his thirteenth birthday. Whether he will make it to that milestone, however, is honestly anybody's guess. I wasn't confident he would even see double digits; every moment with him since then has felt like a gift.

You see, Tex is not in the best of health. In fact, he has a laundry list of ailments as long as his feather-duster fluffy tail. Tex has arthritis, an anxiety disorder, hypothyroidism, leukaemia, epilepsy and an incurable lung disease called bronchiectasis.

The arthritis makes him limp; the anxiety makes him worry and whine; the hypothyroidism causes him to gain weight and makes him more susceptible to other conditions like dermatitis; the leukaemia makes his blood do crazy things; the epilepsy causes violent seizures, almost always in the middle of the night; and the bronchiectasis makes him cough constantly. He has also become deaf in recent years.

On any given day, Tex takes at least twelve pills – more if he's dealing with other issues, which frequently crop up. As I write this, for example, he's also taking two different antibiotics for a nasty abscess that infected his lip after he bit through it during a seizure. I'm at the local vet with Tex at least once a week, either for a routine blood draw (required for the management of his leukaemia), to collect medication, or for the treatment of some new health catastrophe that has blindsided us. And that doesn't even include the visits to the specialist vet hospital. Their eyes light up every time my furry medical mystery saunters through the door; Tex is exactly the kind of puzzle they live for.

Recently, Tex's regular vet casually told me how much money I've spent there in the three years he's been looking after him. Let's just say I needed a stiff drink and a lie down afterwards. Thank Dog for pet insurance.

Some of Tex's health issues are related to his advancing age, but the thing is that Tex has been an old man all his life. He had old dog problems even as a young dog: his arthritis was diagnosed at three, the thyroid disease at five and the anxiety at six. The epilepsy and leukaemia both arrived at eleven, and the lung condition was diagnosed at twelve.

Physical health aside, Tex has had the world-weary crankiness of a much older soul since day one. When he was a youngster, if he was feeling particularly content in whichever spot he was napping, Tex would let out long, dramatic groans that seemed to say, 'Oh, woe! The world is a harsh and unforgiving place!' They became known in our house as his 'old man noises', and I've since learned from other Toller owners that they're a common quirk of the breed.

My family has had to make plenty of accommodations for Tex, both financially and in the way we live day to day. For example, we have to walk him separately from our two younger dogs, because he can't walk as far or as fast as them. And when we go on holiday, given his age and medical history, we don't want to ship him off to the boarding kennel anymore, so we either have to take him with us or find a trusted person who's willing to look after him in our home. And, of course, he continues to cost us plenty of money, although that's no fault of his.

He hasn't been an easy dog, but he has been a perfect dog – a constant joy. And now that he is actually an old dog, chronologically as well as spiritually, I feel an entirely new depth of love for him. He has given me the best of himself and I view it as a great privilege that I am now able to return the favour. I can make sure his remaining time here is as happy, comfortable and love-filled as he deserves.

Tex inspired this book when I realised one day that not everybody would see him that way – that some people would see caring for an ailing and elderly dog as a burden rather than a reward.

I was diligently searching through all the foodstuffs in my fridge, trying to find something in which I could conceal a pill so that Tex would swallow it. Usually I wrap his medication in bits of cheese and he wolfs it down no problem, but every now and then he will decide that he hates cheese and has always hated cheese and how could I be so dense as to imagine he has ever liked cheese? He does this, I think, purely for the fun of it. He likes to keep me on my toes.

Finally we agreed on pepperoni. The medication was duly ingested, and Tex returned to his busy schedule of napping in the most awkward and inconvenient places he can find. As I watched him meander away, it hit me: *So many people would not bother with you.*

So many people would not spend the money it takes to manage Tex's medical issues, even when they could afford it. So many people would not be prepared to change their lifestyle to ensure consistency and comfort for an elderly dog whose health and happiness depend on it. So many people would not see the value in loving a coughing, wheezing, limping dog who does little besides farting and sleeping for twenty hours a day.

For some, it comes down to perceived quality of life. How can a dog like Tex, with his collection of serious illnesses, possibly enjoy his days? That's such an easy question to answer. Tex has medication that ensures he's not in pain and doesn't feel unwell, and a team of vets dedicated to maintaining that. But more importantly, I know he still enjoys life because I know *him*. I've been by his side since he was twelve weeks old. When Tex has had enough, I will know. When he is ready to go, he will either go or ask me to help him move on. When you have loved a dog his entire life, you learn to communicate without words.

Of course, the idea that old equals miserable is pervasive in our society. You need only take a visit to your local shelter or peruse a pet-adoption site to understand that elderly pets are not valued as they should be, just as elderly people are not valued as they should be.

Dogs are dumped when they grow old and lose that puppy playfulness; dumped when their joints ache and they don't want to walk anymore; dumped when their health starts to decline and the vet bills start to grow; dumped when their owner dies or moves into a care facility and there are no relatives or friends willing or able to assume responsibility.

In a way, some of those dumped dogs are the lucky ones. They have a chance at finding a loving home in which to spend their golden years. Many others are simply euthanised when they grow old and people start to think of them as burdensome.

It is such a betrayal, such a cruel reversal for a creature whose chief mission in life has been to love us above all else. As some clever person once noted, a dog spends the majority of his time simply waiting for his human to come home. We are all they want. They may not be our whole world, but we are certainly theirs. Someone even cleverer put it a little more bluntly: if you're not prepared to be there at the end, don't be there at the beginning.

The irony is that discarding an old dog is not only unforgivably disloyal, it's also a great loss to the human. Somebody that has never known the love of an elderly canine has willfully forfeited the velvety soft touch of a greying muzzle, the sound of plodding paws in the hall, the occasional mad burst of puppy-like energy, the beatific expression on an old dog's face as she finds the perfect sunny spot in the garden to while away the afternoon. Imagine choosing to miss out on those sublime moments.

When I realised there are people out there who would not look at Tex the way I do, who would not *love* him the way I do, I knew I needed to write a book that would show just how extraordinary old dogs are.

Old dogs are smart – their capacity and desire for learning does not diminish with age, despite that old adage about old dogs and new tricks. They are soft and gentle, loving and devoted. They are as familiar and comforting as a pair of well-worn slippers. I make no claim to objectivity when I say they are just the absolute best.

The old dogs in this book are truly remarkable. They have saved lives, inspired stunning artworks, survived great hardship, returned home against all odds, and simply kept on keeping on, year after wonderful year. But an old dog doesn't need to do anything noteworthy to be extraordinary. They only need to love fiercely and be loved in return.

Over the course of his long life, Tex has taught me so much about love, friendship and loyalty. My little old puppy, with his million diseases and countless strange habits, will always be one of the great loves of my life.

Loving an old dog is different, certainly, but it is a unique and beautiful chapter in the story of their life. Never forget what an honour it is to be there to share it.

Laura Greaves
July 2020

Haole

The dog who walked on water

The Pacific Ocean archipelago of Hawaii is known for a great many things. It is the USA's only island state, for a start, and the only state located outside of North America. It's famous as a land of volcanic peaks, lush jungles, idyllic beaches and vibrant Polynesian culture. It is also revered as the birthplace of surfing, and its iconic breaks and big waves attract surfers from all across the globe.

In the indigenous tongue of the Hawaiian islands, the word 'haole' (pronounced '*how*-lee') means a foreigner or non-Polynesian person. Locals sometimes direct it at tourists, and not always in a friendly fashion.

It's a little ironic, then, that a senior Labrador named Haole was not only one of the friendliest creatures on four legs, but was as natural on a surfboard as any native Hawaiian.

Haole was the adored firstborn 'son' of Kim Murphy

and her husband, John, who live in sunny California but have close connections to both Hawaii and surfing.

'My dad moved to Hawaii about fifteen years ago, and we just love it,' says Kim. 'John and I travelled to Hawaii with some friends and ended up falling in love with it, getting married there in 2006. Every time we'd go visit, my dad's local friends would say, "The haoles are coming!"'

Travel has always been a big part of the couple's life. John works as a heavy equipment operator and site supervisor in the construction industry, while Kim has worked as a dental assistant at the same thriving orthodontic practice for more than thirty years. At the end of every week, the hardworking Murphys would hit the road to explore California and beyond, with their weekend jaunts often taking them to the beaches in the state's south.

It was on one of these getaways that John presented Kim with a gift that would change both of their lives. 'He surprised me on our anniversary about fifteen years ago with surfing lessons on one of our road trips.'

Kim had grown up in northern California, where she enjoyed waterskiing on the region's lakes and rivers, but she admits she had been intimidated by the notion of surfing until that moment.

'It was mainly because of the fear factor. I was nervous about injuring myself or struggling or looking like a complete idiot. There were a lot of young people that did it, and we got into it later in life,' she says. 'But I fell in love with it, John fell in love with it, and we've been surfing ever since. We became friends with the surfing community and it became a really fun, social thing where I felt really comfortable.'

Haole, whose name was of course inspired by the Murphys' love of Hawaii, joined the family in July 2008. From day one, he loved his weekend trips every bit as much as his owners. 'We got Haole when he was twelve weeks old and he started going to the beach with us right away. John and I took turns surfing and playing with him on the beach. We did that for years.'

Haole's arrival had been a long time coming, though both Kim and John are lifelong dog lovers. Kim's family always had a pooch or two, and when she met John twenty-five years ago he had a young golden retriever called Shane.

'Shane was wonderful. John had him until Shane was about fourteen, and he was such an incredible dog that it took us about four years before we decided we were ready to get another dog,' she says. 'When we first saw Haole he was just super cute. We don't have kids, so Haole became our child.'

And like any child who wants to emulate his parents, young Haole soon decided he wanted to get in on their hobby. In 2013, shortly before his fifth birthday, the lively Lab 'announced' that he wanted to try surfing, too.

'I was playing with him on Ventura beach when John surfed in on a wave and Haole went out to greet him, but then we realised he was actually trying to get up on John's surfboard,' says Kim. 'John tried to put him on the board, but it was too narrow and unstable because Haole weighed 43 kilograms. The next day John brought out a bigger board and straight away Haole was comfortable on it.'

The Murphys were astonished by their bold barker's natural aptitude on the board. They had never heard of a surfing dog before – though they would soon discover there's a whole world of hounds that love to hang ten – so their only focus was ensuring Haole was safe and having fun.

'John just started pushing him on waves. Haole wasn't secured to the board and he didn't try to get off. He was just calm and comfortable,' she says. 'He started drawing a crowd. People on the beach were like, "Oh my God! That's amazing – he's not scared at all!"' The incredible surfing dog was soon a weekend fixture on Ventura beach.

It wasn't long before an impressed onlooker told Kim that there were actual dog surfing competitions for wave-riding canines just like Haole. 'We entered one a few months after Haole started surfing and he won. We started competing regularly after that. There were three or four dog surfing competitions, so we started doing those,' says Kim.

Kim, John and now Haole's passion for surfing soon became so consuming that, in 2014, the trio made the permanent move from California's Santa Clarita Valley to the laidback beach town of Ventura, about 110 kilometres from downtown Los Angeles, so they could hit the waves as often as possible.

'Haole would get so excited when he saw his surfboard. Weather permitting, we'd try to get our boys to the beach every weekend [a second Labrador, Primo, joined the family in 2015] whether to paddleboard or for Haole to surf,' says Kim. 'On days when there was no surf John would paddle with Haole and I'd play fetch on the beach with Primo.'

Not long after their move, the Ventura Visitors and Convention Bureau heard about Haole. 'When we moved out here the visitors' centre just loved Haole's nature and how calm he was and how he loved to surf, and they asked if he could be the ambassador for Ventura. We said, "Of course!"'

And then came another request. The organisers of Surf Rodeo, an annual surf and music festival held at Ventura Pier, asked Kim and John if Haole might do a surfing demonstration. It promised to be a fun weekend and another chance for their beloved boy to make people smile.

They never could have imagined it would lead to a meeting that would change their lives – and the lives of dozens of kids.

It had been a tough day for Jacob Morgan. The active eight-year-old, who has autism, loves to surf. In fact, Jacob had spoken his very first words while riding the waves, after being non-verbal until the age of five.

Today, however, Jacob wasn't feeling it. He didn't want to surf anymore, and he didn't want people trying to encourage him into the ocean. But he wasn't able to express these feelings in words. Instead, Jacob grew increasingly agitated, shouting and lashing out at those who tried to help him calm down.

There were dozens of people on Ventura beach that day, but nobody was fazed by Jacob's challenging behaviour. That's because Jacob was there with A Walk on Water (AWOW), a non-profit organisation that runs surf therapy events for children and adults with special needs and disabilities. Surf therapy pairs guided surf instruction – provided by trained Surf Therapists – with a support network of volunteers, siblings, family and friends. From March to November, events are held at beaches across the United States, treating whole families to a day of respite that includes healthy food and drink, live music, art, yoga, and more.

Since its inception in 2012, the organisation has worked with more than 1000 families and 2000 surfers, all of whom are called athletes. The AWOW team aspires to ulti-mately reach 1500 children per year. Their aim is to help athletes like Jacob 'experience the stoke' of surfing, increasing their self-confidence and pride through accom-plishing a sometimes scary goal, as well as improving interaction with peers and adults in a positive and support-ive environment.

Kim, John and Haole became involved with AWOW after watching a surf therapy demonstration at the Surf Rodeo event in which their attention-grabbing dog was also participating.

'AWOW asked us if we would bring Haole to their event in Ventura a week later, so that's what we did. We knew the kids would love watching him surf, but they actually fell *in* love with him,' says Kim. 'They were hugging him on the beach. They were going in the water purely because Haole was in there.

'They asked us to come back for the next couple of events because the families were asking, "Is Haole going to be there?" It was very organic and wonderful.'

The Morgan family was one of those that was instantly charmed by Haole. When Jacob spotted him on the beach that difficult day, his earlier crankiness vanished. 'When Jacob met Haole, he was immediately like, "I want to walk the dog,"' Kim says. 'So he and I went walking with Haole on the beach. He walked Haole all day long. He didn't even want to surf.'

Soon after that transformative day, Jacob's mum, Jennifer, called Kim. 'She said, "It was really amazing to meet you, because we've never seen this side of Jacob. He was actually very content just being with Haole. He keeps saying he wants to see the dog,"' she recalls.

'After that, when Jacob came to the events, he would immediately come to Haole. Pretty soon, Jacob only wanted to surf if he could surf on the board with Haole.' Kim says Jacob's parents firmly believe that their son's connection with Haole has been deeper and more significant for him than even his relationships with some of his human therapists.

Now fourteen, Jacob has progressed from eschewing all physical contact to hugging Kim and John whenever he sees them at the beach. 'He hugs us; he's happy to see us. It's like a whole new world has opened up with us and our family because of Haole,' says Kim. 'They had a very strong connection. It turned into something really pretty miraculous.'

In fact, Jacob and Haole were so devoted to each other that, initially, Jacob had difficulty sharing his four-legged friend with other athletes.

'The other athletes had seen Haole surf with Jacob and were like, "We want to surf with Haole, too!"' says Kim. 'At first Jacob was really upset about it because he was like, "That's my dog! That's what *we* do!"'

But Kim and John made sure that any athlete who wanted to surf with Haole got a turn on the board with him.

'One of the boys with Down syndrome was very fearful of surfing, but he would always go and sit on Haole's board in the water with him. He was very confident to be in the water with Haole,' she says. 'There's another little boy who has a very severe epileptic condition and he actually referred to Haole as "his" Haole.'

Another young athlete, Xander, was asked to draw a picture of his hero as part of a school project. Xander drew Haole and won a prize for his efforts. 'It was pretty remarkable,' says Kim.

Just what was it about Haole that enabled him to connect so profoundly with AWOW's young athletes? He was an old soul long before he was literally an old dog, says Kim, and his peaceful personality and soothing presence seemed to resonate with differently abled children.

'He just had a great demeanour. A lot of the kids have Down syndrome or autism, and many of them are very scared of dogs in general, but they were confident with

Haole because he didn't react,' she explains. 'When they approached him, he wouldn't try to lick them. If they pulled his tail, he wouldn't react. Kids have stuck their fingers in his nose, pulled his ears . . . nothing!'

Interestingly, Haole's Labrador brother, Primo, who arrived when Haole was seven, is his polar opposite in terms of temperament.

'Primo is very sweet and loving, but he's just a crazy Lab. He's very high energy and he always wants to play. So many families have asked, "When's Primo going to come to an event?" But Primo doesn't have the same personality.' Kim laughs. 'He'd be running all over the beach. If a kid tried to hug him he'd be licking their face. He just doesn't have that *thing* that Haole had. When Haole was on the beach at those events, and we'd stand back and watch him, he knew he was there for a reason. He had a purpose, and the kids really responded to it.'

From casually going along to their first surf-therapy event six years ago, AWOW is today as integral a part of the Murphys' lives as surfing itself. Kim is now the organisation's secretary, while John is an AWOW ambassador and a key member of the surf therapy and water safety teams.

Haole, of course, was AWOW's official 'ambassadog.' He retired from competitive dog surfing in 2016.

Kim says the couple is frequently blown away by how much their adored dog achieved. 'Everything revolved around Haole and this work. Sometimes we'd sit back and think, *Oh my god, this is our dog!* People loved our dog and he actually made a difference in people's lives.

It made me feel very fortunate to be able to do this work with him.'

Haole's ability to inspire transcended his role with AWOW. His Instagram account (@haoleboysurfs) now has more than 32,000 fans and his website offers a range of Haole Boy merchandise. He was even the subject of a 2019 children's book, Margaret O'Hair's *Ride the Wave: Love Sofia and Haole the Surf Dog*, about his bond with Sofia Sanchez, a young AWOW athlete who has Down syndrome.

One of AWOW's guiding principles is that 'it takes a village', and Kim says she and John have been humbled by the village that has embraced them and their adventurous Labrador.

'It's amazing how this has all happened because of our dog. He changed our lives for sure,' says Kim. 'It's opened up doors for us and it's actually just really enlightened us in a way where we can see the good in the world.'

And the support of that village was never more evident – or more desperately needed – than on one dark day in August 2018.

The day Haole was diagnosed with cancer.

Kim and John have always been proactive about their dogs' health. In 2015, when Haole turned seven and officially became a senior dog, the couple decided to implement an annual blood test as part of his routine veterinary care. The first test showed that Haole had an elevated liver enzyme count. His vet wasn't overly worried; Haole wasn't displaying any concerning symptoms. But the result meant he was more susceptible to developing Cushing's disease in later life. The vet added a liver ultrasound to his yearly check-up for good measure.

On the day of his annual physical in 2018, Haole's vet decided to ultrasound the area around his liver as well. There was no particular reason to do so; she just had a hunch. 'When she checked his sublumbar area, she found really enlarged and irregular lymph nodes. It was an anal gland tumour that had metastasised,' Kim says.

Haole was ten years old and had shown no signs of being unwell. The tumour would never have been found if not for his vet's instinct.

Two years on, the shock of the moment she got the devastating news remains fresh for Kim. 'When the vet came in she had this look on her face that scared me. I thought she was going to tell me he had liver disease. She said, "The liver is fine, but . . ." I felt like I stopped breathing. I gasped and said, "Are you telling me he has cancer?" I just lost it and started bawling. All I kept thinking was, *How am I going to tell John that Haole has cancer?*'

The good news was that Haole's was a slow-progressing type of cancer. He would have surgery to remove the tumour in his bottom, as well as the affected lymph nodes in his sublumbar region, and if he made it through then his prognosis would be positive. The removal of the lymph nodes was risky, though: they were located next to major blood vessels and the slightest nick could cause Haole to bleed to death. Haole's surgeon put his chances of survival at fifty-fifty.

Although she felt afraid, Kim says she felt a strong conviction all along that Haole would be okay. Even on the day of his operation, when the surgery that was expected to go for five to six hours dragged out to nine hours, she was confident her much-loved Labrador would pull through.

'I can honestly say that at the time I didn't think he was going to die, but I did think it was going to end everything we did together. I felt like our whole world was going to turn upside down,' she says. 'But when we brought him home after the surgery, I thought, *He's going to get through this – I just don't know how long it's going to take.*'

After surgery, Haole also had a course of radiation in a bid to shrink his secondary tumours.

'With the type of cancer he had, we knew he could easily have a couple more years. What I really appreciated about his doctors was that they were all about taking extreme measures to keep him healthy, but for the right reasons. They told us that when it got to the point where it wasn't worth it anymore they'd tell us.'

And there was no doubt that it definitely *was* worth it. The Murphys threw everything they could at Haole's cancer, because they appreciated that he was not just their dog. He belonged to the entire AWOW community and, in a sense, to the entire world. They were unapologetic about doing everything in their power for their cherished old boy.

'People who aren't animal or dog people just don't get

how you can look at this dog like he's your family, your child, and do anything for him.'

Haole's AWOW family was understandably heartbroken by his diagnosis, but in his six years with the organisation he had missed just a handful of events, and only because they clashed with his cancer treatment. (He also had a forced hiatus in 2020, when AWOW temporarily suspended its events due to the COVID-19 pandemic.)

Aside from that, right up until he was twelve years old, Haole was on the beach with his beloved AWOW athletes every chance he got. Labradors live ten to fourteen years on average, so the fact that Haole was still surfing at the age of twelve would have been impressive even without his cancer battle.

Haole drew people to AWOW events just so they could meet him, and he became an unlikely beacon of hope for other cancer sufferers. 'Every single event, we met somebody who follows Haole on Instagram who had come just to meet him,' says Kim. 'One woman came up to us in New Jersey and said, "I don't want you guys to think I'm crazy, but I had to come and meet Haole because I found out I had cancer at the same time he was diagnosed."

'I was blown away. This was a grown woman, and she had come to meet my dog because they both had cancer. She said, "This is the best day ever. I can't believe I'm meeting him. My life is complete." It was amazing.'

It's these serendipitous moments that helped Kim and John remain positive as Haole fought on. It was business as usual for Haole for as long as possible.

'We tried very hard to be strong and to keep up the positive energy around the house. We did not live our lives like he had cancer. We were always going to do our normal thing,' she says.

Through it all, Kim was astonished by Haole's resilience and undimmed lust for life. She says people were often surprised to learn of Haole's advanced age, let alone that he'd had major surgery and had cancer. 'He didn't look like an old man. People asked us how old he was and when we'd tell them that he was twelve they'd say, "Oh my gosh, you're kidding me – I thought he was a puppy!" Everybody was just blown away,' she says.

'I can't believe how he rebounded from everything he'd been through. He just seemed to bounce back and keep going.'

John, on the other hand, was a little more nonchalant. Not only about his dog's tenacity in the face of adversity, but also the impact Haole had on so many lives.

'I'm still blown away all the time,' says Kim. 'People bonded with Haole without even knowing him, just from seeing the photos or the videos of him surfing with the kids. I'm like, *He's just this dog that we fell in love with!* But John was like, *Yeah, of course this happened. It's Haole.*'

Sadly, by May 2020, Haole was no longer able to bounce back. On 13 May he passed away in his backyard, on his beloved surfboard, surrounded by love. It was twenty-one months to the day after his cancer diagnosis.

A heartbroken Kim wrote to his Instagram followers: 'If I described everything about Haole – his personality; his giving heart; his old, soulful eyes; his temperament; his love, guidance, commitment, dedication, bravery, smile, surfing ability, accomplishments, brotherhood, companionship; his organic ability to form long-lasting relationships – literally I could go on and on.'

Every moment with Haole was a gift, but from the moment he stepped on a surfboard, life has been an adventure the Murphys never could have anticipated. Even now, as she and John mourn his passing, Kim says she never loses sight of how profoundly Haole shaped and enriched their existence.

'There will be no other like him. He may no longer live on this earth, but he will forever live in our hearts, and the hearts of everyone that he met,' she says. 'We are eternally grateful for all that have entered our lives because of Haole, and we will continue to live on the path he laid.'

Without their incredible old dog, chances are Kim and John wouldn't have embraced the sport of surfing quite so passionately. They wouldn't have begun working with A Walk on Water. They wouldn't have been instrumental in putting smiles on the faces of so many children.

'We've had some really wonderful things happen because of this one bad thing. Haole had cancer, yet we've had some really amazing things come out of that because he just touched even more people's hearts,' she says. 'He had his own battle and yet he still gave to others. We've met some wonderful people that we wouldn't have in our lives if things hadn't turned in this direction.'

The American author Agnes Sligh Turnbull once said, 'Dogs' lives are too short; their only fault, really.' But few dogs packed as much into their lives as Haole Boy the surfing dog. He may now be surfing waves in dog heaven, but Haole changed countless lives and for that he will be remembered forever.

And that makes him immortal.

Maggie

The oldest dog in the world

If there's one thing about dogs and ageing that everyone knows, it's this: one year of a dog's life is equivalent to seven human years.

We all agree that when Fido blows out the candle on his first birthday cake, he is at the same level of physical maturity as a seven-year-old child. Every subsequent year is worth another seven human trips around the sun, so if he makes it to twelve years old, he's eighty-four in people terms. Those rare good boys and girls that make it into their teens are pushing 100 human years – a good innings in anybody's estimation.

We all seem to absorb this tidbit of dog trivia from the ether, and few of us ever question it. But here's the thing: it's not true.

It's hard to pinpoint where the 'dog years' myth began; it seems to have been around forever. But for as long as it has existed, veterinarians and other canine experts have been trying to debunk it. The truth is that all dogs age differently, and according to a heap of varying factors, including breed, size and overall health.

In reality, a ten-year-old Chihuahua has aged to about the same extent as a 56-year-old person, while a Bulldog at ten would be around sixty-five in human years. Meanwhile, a Great Dane that has clocked up a decade of good living is roughly equivalent to a 75-year-old biped.

The one-year-equals-seven equation also cannot account for those very special dogs that reach twenty or older. If the myth were correct, it would mean a twenty-year-old pooch's body had weathered 140 years of wear and tear. While that would be amazing, it's very unlikely, if not impossible.

Well, impossible except for a Victorian kelpie named Maggie.

When Maggie passed away on her owner Brian McLaren's dairy farm in April 2016, he believes she was at least *thirty* years old. (We might once have said that was 210 in human years, but now we know better.) He can no longer prove exactly how old she was – we'll get to that – but officially speaking or not, her astonishingly lengthy life probably makes Maggie the longest-lived dog in the world.

Brian has been a dairy farmer in Woolsthorpe, in southern Victoria, all his life; the farm has been in his family for four generations. He's had working dogs all his life, too. They help to move and corral the cattle, and they're tireless toilers who love every moment of it.

Some of his dogs have had more aptitude for the job than others, though. 'I've always had dogs, some successful and some unsuccessful. A successful dog is one that's got a really good temperament, is not aggressive, and is easily trained,' Brian says. 'If they're a bit scatterbrained and you can't control them, they're not much good for dairy cows.'

In the early nineties, the farm dog was Jack the black-and-tan kelpie, whose enthusiasm for rounding up cattle was unmatched by any of Brian's previous dogs. As soon as he heard 'go back' – his instruction to go and bring the cows from the paddock to the dairy for milking – he'd be off like a shot.

'Jack would go anywhere for cows, especially in the morning. We'd go out the door at 5 a.m. and he'd be right there. We'd tell him to "go back" and he'd disappear into the darkness, and by the time I got into the dairy, all the cows would be there,' he says.

Sadly, Jack's promising career was curtailed by a shocking accident. He was struck by a milk tanker and died when he was only about five years old. The loss was so devastating that Brian vowed never to have another working dog; he would herd the cattle on his motorbike rather than risk such grief again.

But his wife, Sue, had other ideas.

'I'd decided that was it – no more dogs for me. I was that upset. But Sue convinced me that I should go and see this guy who had dogs advertised that he couldn't get rid of,' he says.

In country terms, the seller was a near neighbour – he lived about 20 kilometres west of Brian's property. Brian decided the purebred kelpies he was advertising were worth a look.

When he met the eight-week-old female puppy, his first impression wasn't so much positive as staggeringly impressed.

'This little puppy was out in the paddock chasing cows. She was just a little ball of fluff, but she was wandering around in the paddock,' says Brian. 'She couldn't do much – the cows were up, looking at her – but she wanted to chase. She was out looking to work. That's what got me over the line with her: she was interested in chasing cows already.'

So it was decided. The McLarens' farm would have another dog after all. It was a lucky break for the puppy in more ways than one – her breeder told Brian that the rest of the litter was destined for an animal shelter, because he didn't know what to do with them.

Brian, Sue and their three sons – Joe, Chris and Liam – bundled the puppy into the car and hit the road. On the drive home, they debated possible names for their new 'employee'. With a minimum of fuss, she was christened Maggie.

One way Brian knows for sure that Maggie lived to be at least thirty is that his youngest son, Liam, wasn't yet at school when Maggie joined the family, so he can't have been more than four years old; Brian actually thinks he may have been even younger. When Maggie passed away in 2016, Liam was thirty-four.

Before long Maggie was a McLaren through and through – and as Brian's first encounter with her had suggested, she was a natural with cows. She was the only working dog he had, because she was the only working dog he needed.

'Dairy farmers usually only have one working dog at a time. Sheep farmers have multiples because they've got to control big mobs of sheep, and it's all about getting them on the truck,' he explains. 'But rounding up cows has got to be gentle, and Maggie was exceptionally gentle. She was one out of the box.'

Laidback and easy to train, Australian kelpies are known for their smarts and indefatigable work ethic. They commonly work with sheep, cattle, goats, pigs and even poultry. Farmers and stockmen say that, when it comes to mustering livestock, one good kelpie can do the work of several hired hands.

Maggie was a shining example of her breed. She had instinct in spades, and being both gentle and highly intelligent she was able to herd cattle with almost no guidance from Brian.

'She didn't take a lot of training. When she was young I could just whistle and send her for the cows. I didn't have to yell and scream at her. She knew what she had to do,' he says. 'I might be in the middle of a ten-hectare paddock on the motorbike and she'd be on the other side, walking behind the cows. We're talking seven hundred cows.'

Maggie quickly developed her own unique way of doing things. While many cattle dogs will bark their charges into formation, she preferred a quieter approach. She liked to make the cows come to *her*.

'When she had to shift a cow, she wouldn't bark. She'd just lie down on her belly and wait for it to walk towards her, and then nip it on the nose,' says Brian. 'The cow would turn and walk away and she'd follow it. She wouldn't bark unless I told her to – she'd wait until I told her to "speak up".'

Maggie also had a competitive streak. While she did her work on four paws, Brian did his on two wheels, mustering and droving the cows on a motorcycle. The machine instantly became Maggie's nemesis.

'Most of our droving is done on a motorbike, and she hated being beaten by the bike. She just *hated* it.' Brian laughs. 'She wouldn't go on the back of the bike – she wanted to run alongside it and race it. She'd disappear and then turn up behind the cows.'

She was fastidious about her work, too, refusing to knock off for the day until every cow was accounted for. 'When she was bringing them home for the night, if I left her on her own she could bring them in by herself. If she missed a couple and it was still daylight, I could send her out again and she'd get the ones she missed.'

It wasn't just cows whose occasional tardiness frustrated Maggie. If her boys – Joe, Chris and Liam – weren't home from school on time, she would vent her spleen to anyone within earshot.

'She knew the kids got home off the school bus at ten past four every afternoon. You could set your watch by her:

every day at 4.10 p.m. she'd go out the front and wait,' says Brian. 'If they weren't on time, she'd bark until they arrived. She did that until well after the kids had grown up and left school.'

And so it went, year after happy year. The seasons changed and changed again, but Maggie's dedication to her job never wavered. Every morning and afternoon she would be raring to bring the cows from their paddock to the dairy and every evening she'd guide them home to bed.

Her only flaw – if it can even be called a flaw – was that Maggie was terrified of thunderstorms. On stormy nights, she had to be secured for her own safety. 'Maggie was never a house dog as such – never inside except during storms. She hated thunder and would run a mile, so she'd get locked up on the back verandah at night.'

Aside from that, the little black-and-tan kelpie was fearless. Nothing fazed her, and she thrived on farm life like she was born for it – which, essentially, she was.

Her connection to the farm was so strong that, in 2000, when Brian and Sue moved from the property to live in the town of Koroit, 15 kilometres away, Maggie wouldn't have a bar of it. (Fun fact: the farm is only 150 kilometres from Casterton, Victoria, renowned as the birthplace of the Australian kelpie breed.)

Brian continued to run the dairy farm in conjunction with tenant farmers, and he had figured Maggie would continue to work there during the day and then come home to the house in town with him at night.

Maggie did not agree with this plan.

'That lasted a week.' Brian laughs. 'I thought she'd live with us at night. Nup – she'd sit under my window and bark all night. She just barked and barked and barked, so she ended up living out at the farm. We had sharefarmers there, so she was well looked after.'

With such an eager and unflagging colleague by his side, Brian never thought much about Maggie's advancing years. She was always there, tail wagging, when Brian arrived at the farm in the wee hours of every morning. Age, it seemed, had not wearied her.

'I'd pull up and open the door to the dairy. It would be dead quiet, and then I'd hear her coming from the office where she slept, looking for her food,' Brian says. 'Kelpies just love working. It's what they like doing. They don't like sitting around.'

Then, one day, an offhand comment from his eldest son, Joe, got Brian thinking.

And running the numbers in his head.

The next thing he knew, it felt like the whole world was talking about Maggie.

As a general rule, the smaller the dog the longer its life. The list of the world's 10 longest-living breeds is a roll call of petite pooches that includes the Chihuahua, Maltese, toy poodle, Jack Russell terrier and Shih tzu.

But there are, of course, exceptions to every rule. According to Guinness World Records, the official oldest dog in the world is none other than a humble Australian kelpie.

His name was Bluey and, like Maggie, he hailed from rural Victoria. He lived with farmer Les Hall on a cattle and sheep property near Rochester. Les obtained Bluey as a puppy in 1910 and he worked the property for well over twenty years. He lived until November 1939, making him an incredible twenty-nine years and five months old.

The average lifespan for the breed is twelve to fifteen years, but there is a wealth of anecdotes about kelpies that have pushed on until closer to twenty.

With his long history of long-living dogs, it's perhaps no surprise that Brian hadn't registered that Maggie was getting on a bit. That is, until Joe remarked one evening that she hadn't really been working for the past ten years.

This was 2015. Joe had joined Brian to work on the farm in 2005, after returning to Victoria from a stint in Western Australia, so he knew Maggie's routines just as well as his father did. He noted that Maggie mostly just 'hung around' these days, having quietly retired from working the cows a decade ago.

When Brian thought about it, he realised his son was right. Because she was still always by his side he hadn't paid much attention, but Maggie had been winding down right before his eyes.

'I didn't take a lot of notice until Joe said that. It had been a gradual thing. Maggie stopped trying to beat the motorbike and was happy to get on the back of it instead,' he says. 'But she'd come to work, and when I'd go home I'd give her a pat and say, "See you tomorrow." It wasn't until she decided she'd had enough of racing the bike that I noticed.'

Soon Maggie's begrudging acceptance of trips on the motorcycle dwindled, too. 'She'd come on the bike if I was going somewhere and sometimes I'd have to lift her on. Then when we got there, she wouldn't get off. That went on for about five years, and then she didn't want to come at all,' says Brian.

He figured she had to be somewhere in the region of twenty-nine years old. The boys started joking that Maggie deserved a medal for sticking around so long. 'It started out as a bit of fun. Joe said we should get Maggie in the *Guinness Book of World Records*. I'd never thought about it until he mentioned it, but suddenly I thought, *Wow, maybe she is pretty old.*'

Trouble was, Brian knew he couldn't prove it. As a purebred puppy, Maggie had come with pedigree papers. They listed her father, a stud dog from Ballarat, and her mother, who had lived with the hapless breeder. But those papers had been lost or discarded in the move from the farm into Koroit. Brian hadn't seen them in fifteen years, and he knew no official body would simply take his word for it.

Still, he thought the story of his lovely old cattle dog might make a nice little snippet for his local newspaper, *The Weekly Times*. The paper's back page was devoted to quirky and feel-good stories from the local area.

'I knew a girl who worked at *The Weekly Times*, so I rang her and said, "I've got a dog that might be thirty years old – would you like to put her on the back page?"' he recalls. 'Later that day, the editor rang me and said, "I think we can do better than that." They turned up to take some photos of Maggie and me, and ended up doing a two-page spread.'

The ink was barely dry when Brian received another phone call, this time from a television journalist at Seven News. He found his dog's sudden celebrity amusing, if a little baffling. 'The guy from Channel Seven rang me and said they wanted a story and I said, "Why? It's only a bloody dog, mate."'

But Maggie wasn't only a dog, not really – and Brian knows it. 'She was easily the best one I've had. If you look her up on the Seven News website the story still comes up,' he says proudly.

Next came interview requests from the northern hemisphere. 'I did a Skype interview with a guy in Canada who writes for the biggest-selling pet magazine in North America,' he says. 'I couldn't believe it.'

One question he was always asked was just *how* Maggie had managed to live to such a ripe old age. To what did Brian attribute her amazing longevity? Was it the fresh country air? The intense daily exercise? Was her water bowl the fountain of youth?

Brian did have an idea of what might have helped Maggie to stay healthy and active for so very long, but it might have made some non-farmers a little squeamish. It turns out that while Maggie's staple diet was dry dog food, she considered cow placenta to be something of a delicacy. It is rich in nutrients and, according to Maggie, pretty tasty to boot.

By the summer of 2016, Maggie's age was noticeably catching up with her. Her lovely face was completely grey and she had become deaf. She stuck close to the farm office, napping in her basket. 'That basket looked as raggedy as she did.' Brian laughs.

But she could still muster up a bit of vim and vigour when the occasion called for it. 'I have a heap of cats at the dairy, to control mice and vermin, and she would always stand over her food and snap and snarl at the cats,' says Brian. 'I'd have to feed her first and she wouldn't take one mouthful until she'd had a go at the cats.'

She was still antagonising the cats come April, which was a relief to Brian. Maggie had declined significantly and he was worried he would soon have to decide whether enough was enough for her. He really didn't want to have to make that choice – how could he possibly call time on such an extraordinary life? To see her still on her feet eased his concern a little.

On 18 April, Maggie ambled from the office to the dairy and back again as usual. She growled at her feline foes, as was her custom. It looked like Maggie, the little kelpie that could, would keep on chugging for a little while yet.

But the next day, Brian could tell something wasn't quite right. Maggie, who usually snoozed the day away, was constantly up and down out of her basket. At day's end, Brian helped her to settle and wished her goodnight. 'She seemed a little bit agitated, so I put her back in her basket and gave her a pat,' he says.

When he arrived at the farm the next morning, Maggie was exactly where Brian had left her. But unlike the 10,000 previous mornings they had spent together, she didn't get up to greet him. Maggie had passed away during the night, peacefully, in her sleep.

Ever the faithful companion, she had spared Brian the agony of having to choose the moment of their farewell. Brian buried Maggie in a marked grave under a pine tree alongside another cherished family dog.

Though Brian knew he'd had more time with Maggie than most people could ever dream of having with their dog, her death hit him hard. 'It was like losing my best friend. I still think of her when I open the door in the morning and I don't hear her coming. Now and again I do say, "I do miss you, you old bitch!"'

Losing Maggie left a hole in the world of the farm, one Brian knows better than to try to fill. 'I haven't had another farm dog since and I haven't wanted to. We've got enough motorbikes and people to not need a dog. It's too hard to replace Maggie.'

Just as Maggie's first foray into the media had made headlines around the world, so too did news of her passing. Major Australian and international news outlets including the ABC, BBC, and *USA Today* aired and posted tributes to Maggie, the unofficial oldest dog who ever lived.

But Maggie's death didn't make Brian feel any need to make the title official. 'It's not something I'm interested in. I loved my dog because she was my dog, not because she was a certain age or had a pedigree,' he explains. 'It doesn't mean anything that she doesn't hold the record. I'm pleased that she still comes up online, but it doesn't bother me at all that it's not official.'

It's testament to the bond they shared that Brian scarcely noticed Maggie's age until she was well and truly elderly. He was too busy working with her, enjoying her company and marvelling at her skill in the paddock to dwell on her seniority. Age, after all, is just a number.

Brian has a pet dog now, Buddy, who's an old fellow as well – he's knocking on fifteen – and is special in his own way. 'Buddy will just sit there and look at me or push his head up under my hand, looking for a scratch. I love old dogs. They're just so lovely and friendly and set in their ways,' Brian says. 'I reckon the older they get the better they get. If they're good dogs they become your best friend, and Maggie was one in a million.'

She certainly was.

Chaser

The dog who could talk

There isn't a dog owner on the planet that hasn't gazed at their four-legged friend at least once and said, 'I wish you could talk.' What would our dogs say if they could speak to us? Would they be chatty and effusive, offering running commentary on the wonders of sunshine on their bellies and naps on the sofa?

Would they ask questions? *Where do you go when you walk out the front door every morning? Why can't I drink out of the toilet?* Maybe they'd be demanding: *Play with me! Scratch my ears! Stop cuddling the cat!* Perhaps they would even be a little ornery, dissatisfied with the frequency of walks and sporadic dispensing of treats.

Most likely they wouldn't say much at all. They would simply look into our eyes and say, 'I love you and I know you love me, too.'

From the time he was a little boy growing up in Memphis,

Tennessee, John Pilley marvelled at dogs' ability to word-lessly communicate with their humans. A childhood incident sparked in John a lifelong interest in the human–animal bond and our attempts to understand each other.

'My father would vacation in rural Mississippi with his Aunt Lillian, who had farm animals and dogs,' says John's daughter, Debbie Pilley-Bianchi, who is widely known as Pilley. 'One summer in the forties, when he was about sixteen, he was standing outside on a Sunday afternoon watching everyone go inside for Sunday dinner. Miss Lillian had a black dog that was not allowed in the house. The dog would move under the house and lie down, every now and then he'd get back up and move to another place, lie back down. He could see that the dog was following his aunt's footsteps in the house above. When she would stop, the dog would stop. That just fascinated him.'

While John became a passionate and lifelong scholar, the notion of pursuing and developing that fascination as a career wouldn't have occurred to him then. In the mid twentieth century, even veterinary medicine was rudimentary by today's standards; animal behavioural science didn't yet exist as a field of professional study.

Besides, John had other fascinations to keep his quick mind occupied. He was deeply interested in religious theology and decided to become a Presbyterian minister. While studying at Princeton Theological Seminary in New Jersey, he met student nurse Sally McFarland. After a whirlwind three-month courtship, they married in 1955 and set up home in Long Island, New York, where they soon welcomed daughters Robin and Debbie, as well as the first of many border collies, Fluffy.

Later, the family moved to Lake Mary, Florida, where John became a pastor. But he felt he struggled to connect with his congregation there. 'He didn't understand them,' says Pilley. 'So at the age of thirty-six he went back to college to study psychology.'

In 1969, John became Memphis State University's first PhD graduate. He wanted to help his parishioners learn more about themselves and their connection with other people and the world. But John's psychology studies also reignited his interest in animal behaviour and communication. Soon he was at the forefront of a burgeoning new area of research.

'He ended up going into behavioural psychology, and that's where his true love lay. He always worked with rats and pigeons in his classroom, and as young children we'd go to the lab with him and play with them. They were really unique creatures and Dad had huge respect for them,' Pilley says.

There were plenty of animals at home, too. Horses and dogs – always collies and collie crosses – were ubiquitous once the Pilleys moved to Spartanburg, South Carolina, in the seventies. 'All of our animals were science fair projects,' she laughs.

When Fluffy passed away, Bimbo joined the family. He was followed by Yasha, a border collie–German shepherd mix who became John's constant companion.

John was an expert white-water kayaker, and often received one of just fifty annual permits issued to elite kayakers by the National Parks Department for running the Grand Canyon rapids. He would take Yasha on multi-day river trips, kitting the dog out with a lifejacket he'd made himself. Yasha rode proudly beside John in his boat, and even learned to body surf.

Yasha's adventurous spirit and eagerness to learn reminded John of the clever dog he'd observed at his Aunt Lillian's house on that steamy Sunday afternoon more than three decades earlier. He began to wonder what else dogs were capable of learning.

'Up until that point, anything Dad had done with dogs was behavioural research, but he believed dogs were way smarter than they'd been given credit for and he wanted to see if he could teach them human language,' Pilley says. 'He wanted to teach them nouns – the names of objects – in the classroom.'

By then working as a professor at Spartanburg's Wofford College, John and his students began to work with Yasha and other dogs in earnest. His goal was to prove that, with training, the canny collie could distinguish the names of objects. He was successful to a point, but soon ran into a roadblock.

'They tried all kinds of methods, and they were successful in teaching the dogs very complex behaviours. In order to get a treat on top of a filing cabinet, for example, the dog would have to drag a chair over to the desk with a rope, and then climb up,' she explains.

'But they could not teach any of the dogs to understand nouns without pairing them with a verb. When Dad asked

Yasha to get the newspaper, he would run out to the mailbox, grab the paper and bring it into the house. Then Dad would ask him to find the newspaper *in* the house, and he could not figure it out. He couldn't isolate the noun from the verb.'

Yasha's confusion is understandable. After all, most of the words we assume our dogs 'know' are in fact tasks or activities – in other words, they're verbs. When we ask, 'Where's your leash?' the word 'leash' may be a noun, but what the dog understands is its function. They recognise the word only in the context of, 'It's time to go for a walk.'

When John retired from Wofford College in 1995, he went into the next phase of his life believing that dogs were brilliant creatures, but they simply could not learn human language.

That was, until Yasha died. His death devastated John, and he couldn't bring himself to get another dog for a long time. Instead, he began to attend sheepdog trials and observe border collies in their element.

'He was fascinated by how in-tune they were with the farmer and the sheep; how accurately they responded to verbal cues. They seemed to be problem solving,' says Pilley. 'We felt from our own experience that border collies were problem solvers, but there was no scientific data to indicate they really could solve problems.'

After a long day's trialling, John said as much to a group of veteran sheep farmers as they relaxed around a campfire. Their dogs were undoubtedly impressive, he told the men, but the science showed they didn't really know their own names and couldn't understand nouns.

There was a heavy silence until one farmer spoke up. 'If that's true,' he said to John, 'then you tell me why I can call Tilly out of my four other dogs and ask him to go and get Bo and Bill, two sheep out of a hundred, and he'll do it every time.'

Pilley recalls that her father was shocked by the man's statement. In an instant, John was forced to rethink everything he thought he knew about canine cognition. 'This floored my dad. He was so humbled and humiliated. He went back to a very basic truth, which is that if learning does not take place, you have to change the method.'

It wasn't that the dogs couldn't learn, John realised. The problem was that his teaching was flawed.

'Some researchers put themselves in a bubble and get very territorial, but my father was a very humble person, and a very curious person. He was not afraid to ask other people's opinions and seek input from unusual sources,' says Pilley. 'He was not afraid to say, "I got it wrong."'

John knew he had to go back to the drawing board and start all over again. And he was about to meet the dog that would help him do it.

By the end of 2003, John's wife, Sally, had had enough of living a dogless existence. She informed her husband that her Christmas gift to him would be a border collie puppy.

John knew exactly where his new puppy pal would come from. For years, working at Wofford College, John would take his psychology students to Flint Hill Farm, a working sheep and horse ranch at Pauline, twenty minutes from downtown Spartanburg. The farm's owner, Wayne West, had been breeding border collies since the sixties. John felt that watching Wayne's dogs work in perfect symbiosis with the livestock was a sight to behold, and a valuable practical lesson for his students.

In May 2004, he chose a four-week-old female pup from Wayne's latest litter. The little dog came home to the Pilley family in June, but didn't have a name for her first month there; John and Sally wanted to get to know their new companion and wait for the perfect moniker to become clear.

That happened the day the wriggling black-and-white bundle ran after a red Jeep; Robin suggested they call her Chaser.

From day one Chaser was 'a real personality', says Pilley. 'Chaser was a love-the-one-you're-with dog. She loved everybody. She was also a manipulator – she was notorious for that. She was *not* an obedient dog.' She laughs. 'She knew her obedience commands, but my father really encouraged her to express herself. She had a very unique relationship with Dad because they were one and the same personality type. He had patience like nobody I've ever seen before. My father was a border collie!'

He started working on Chaser's vocabulary when she was just eight weeks old. A staunch proponent of the power of the human–animal bond, John always advocated training dogs one-on-one.

'When researchers work with animals that they have no real connection with, it means they're missing out on that bond that animals can develop with humans,' Pilley says. 'My father firmly believed that the greatest leaps in animal science are made when we work one-on-one.'

His re-evaluation of his work after his conversation with the farmers had led to something of an epiphany for John: for an animal to learn the name of an object, the object had to have value.

'People have great memory systems, but not when we don't care about something. It's the same with dogs: if the object has value, the word has value,' Pilley explains. 'Take "bath" – it doesn't take long for them to figure out if they like it or don't like it!'

John was determined to set Chaser up to succeed, so he implemented a teaching method called errorless learning, which means creating an environment in which she cannot fail. He would choose an object young Chaser coveted – her blue ball – and ensure success was her only option. He taught her using a mix of verbal cues, visual cues and imitation.

'The blue ball would be the only object on the floor – there were no other toys, so she couldn't get confused. Dad would pick it up and say, "Chaser, this is blue." He'd roll it and say, "Catch blue." And then, "Find blue." He'd hide the ball in plain sight so she could not make a mistake.'

He would repeat this process in short spurts over several days. John soon learned that, like most dogs, Chaser's love of repetition could only be exhausted by John's own exhaustion, and he didn't want to wear either of them out with too much testing.

After three days, when Chaser could identify the colour blue in another room, John moved on to the next object. By the time she was five months old, Chaser could identify 200 different objects by name.

Then came a big leap in her cognition, says Pilley. 'She had that "Aha!" moment. Dad said, "Chaser, this is . . ." and a light switched on in her brain: *Oh! When he holds that up, the word belongs to the object!* After that she could learn things in one try.'

Chaser's realisation meant she had mastered a concept. 'My father believed that learning one concept was infinitely greater than learning one hundred behaviours, because learning builds upon learning.'

After that, the floodgates opened. Chaser went from learning the names of individual objects, such as a ball, to learning that a ball is round and bouncy, and being able to identify other round and bouncy things as balls.

She understood categories of objects, and knew the difference between one to many and many to one. For example, she understood that 'car' could be anything that had four wheels and zoomed down the road, or *the* car in the driveway.

Chaser also knew words that quantified, such as bigger and smaller. 'All of this was layered learning for Chaser. It was built into play. On their walks, Dad would say, "Chaser, this is a tree – go to tree," and gradually he was able to say,

"Chaser, find a tree," and she would find a new one. Or he would say, "Find a bigger stick," and she would go get a bigger one."

Her understanding of human language also meant that Chaser could use it for her own benefit. She may not have been able to use words herself, but she was certainly able to express her opinions to her family – with frequently hilarious results.

'She would organically learn things we didn't even realise she was learning. We were sitting around the kitchen table one night and Mom said, "I'm not going to take Chaser for a walk today because Casey [another dog] is in town and I don't think Chaser likes Casey." Chaser immediately came up to the table and started growling,' Pilley recalls. 'I looked over and said, "Chaser, you don't like Casey?" and she started barking. We went through about six people and dogs, and Chaser had a very distinct reaction to each one. Casey always elicited a growl or a bark.

'She reached a point where if we asked, "Do you want to go?" she would sit up and look at us, like, *Tell me where we're going first*. If we were going to the store, she'd lay back down. She was really able to communicate what she liked and didn't like, where she wanted to go or wanted us to go.'

Perhaps surprisingly, given John was seeing his life's work come to fruition, Pilley says she didn't fully appreciate just how remarkable Chaser's and her father's achievements really were.

'I knew that what he was doing was important, but Chaser was still the family dog. I didn't have a clue that what she was doing was so amazing, and I don't even think my parents understood the global impact his work would have,' she says. 'The way she could combine those words exceeded the work that had been done teaching language to primates and dolphins. She was really one of the icons of animal cognition, along with Alex, a grey parrot known for his intelligent use of speech, and Kanzi, the bonobo who learned language by using keyboard lexigrams.'

It was her ability to go beyond simply memorising words and actually pair verbs with nouns – to understand the building blocks of sentences – that brought Chaser to wider public attention.

Though he had retired from Wofford College nearly a decade before, John had remained associated with the college as an emeritus professor. Among other activities, he worked with varsity athletes on performance psychology, at their coaches' request. In turn, Wofford made its facilities available to John for his research with Chaser.

The two would work together for up to five hours a day, five days a week. But while it may sound like a gruelling schedule, Pilley says Chaser's wellbeing was always John's priority. 'My father viewed Chaser as his partner. What she wanted to do was just as valuable as what he wanted to do. David Johnson, a legendary dog breeder on the US east coast, told my father, "If you give a dog your heart they will give you their mind." That was Dad's motto. If Chaser was not having fun, he stopped.'

*

In 2010, when Chaser was six, John published his findings in collaboration with Wofford psychology professor Dr Alliston Reid in the prestigious academic journal *Behavioural Processes*. The study revealed that Chaser could identify and retrieve 1022 different objects by name. That's three times more than the average toddler, meaning she had the largest tested 'vocabulary' of any non-human animal.

The study caused a stir in the academic community, then captured the attention of the mainstream media. It rapidly led to international recognition for John and Chaser. Within forty-eight hours, articles and broadcast reports about the pair had appeared in seventy-two languages. People all over the world were amazed and enthralled by the professor and his incredible 'talking' dog. Brian Hare, a renowned anthropologist from Duke University, called Chaser 'the most important dog in the history of modern scientific research'.

Even as she aged, Chaser's thirst for learning never seemed to diminish. By 2014, she was ten years old – a senior dog by any official or unofficial measure – but she continued to charm and impress everyone she met. That year, celebrated journalist Anderson Cooper came to meet John and Chaser for the current affairs show *60 Minutes*. The segment, called 'The Smartest Dog in the World', proved to be one of the most popular in the show's history.

Pilley was present for the filming at her parents' house, and once again found herself marvelling at Chaser's abilities – as well as her slightly diva-esque demands. 'She did her language learning demonstration, but that kind of thing was tedious for her. I let the crew know, "You have two takes to get this right, because Chaser will do it again, but she will look bored and hangdog." She'd be like, *Alright, I'll do it, but why do I have to?*' She laughs.

Eventually, Chaser dug her paws in and refused to continue. 'She had performed beautifully on camera and we were taking a break. Chaser was in the middle of the backyard, just staring at Denise, the producer, who kept calling her to come. Chaser just sat there.

'My sister, Robin, was there, and Denise finally said, "Why isn't she doing what I ask?" Robin said, "She's just spent forty-five minutes doing something for you and now she wants you to do something for her – she wants you to engage with her; to chase her and throw the ball." As soon as Denise did that, Chaser was happy to do as she asked.'

In addition to the *60 Minutes* piece, John was interviewed by media outlets far and wide about his amazing dog. Australia's *60 Minutes* team also travelled to the US to meet Chaser in 2016, and she charmed veteran journalist Liz Hayes.

'It's really incredible to see all the publications,' says Pilley. 'We have articles from Russia, South America, all over Europe, South Korea, Japan. It reminds me of how, really, Chaser belongs to the world. It just shows how much people love their own dogs.'

Such was the interest in Chaser and the demand for demonstrations of her talent, Pilley and John briefly considered training the brainy border collie to be a Hollywood star, in the vein of Lassie or Rin Tin Tin.

'CBS, the network that screens *60 Minutes*, wanted her to come to Hollywood. They had a show called *Scorpion* that was about geniuses and they thought, *Let's have a genius dog!*' Pilley says. 'I think Chaser would have been great, and she would have loved it, but she was a senior dog by then. I told them, "You don't need a genius dog to play a genius dog on TV."'

Chaser was even the subject of a successful book, *Chaser: Unlocking the Genius of the Dog Who Knows a Thousand Words*, which John co-authored with Hilary Hinzmann.

A *New York Times* bestseller and the possibility of a silver screen career certainly brought home to Pilley just how exceptional her family dog was. 'It's kind of mind-blowing to think that Chaser's accomplishments have turned her into a global phenomenon. And that Dad's methodology of teaching, at least here in the US, is turning dog training on its ear. More and more, people are using these kinds of methods to foster new learning and really take advantage of this bond that we have with dogs.'

Through all their one-on-one work and worldwide acclaim, what always shone through was John and Chaser's deep connection. In 2016, Wofford College awarded John an honorary degree for his work on animal cognition. Chaser, of course, attended the conferment ceremony with him.

*

Sadly, their connection came to an end in 2018. John was diagnosed with leukaemia in late April of that year and passed away on 17 June, just two weeks before his ninetieth birthday.

The Pilleys have always been a close-knit clan, and John's passing left a void. But he gave his children – and, it seems, his dogs – a great gift: a deep love of learning.

'My dad had the philosophy that every five years he needed to learn something new. In his forties it was flat-water canoeing, then white-water kayaking. He built our family home himself in 1984. He was a lifelong learner,' says Pilley.

'Even when we were young he would get up when we got up and go to McDonald's to study. What was marvellous was that he was always very present. He was always engaged with his children's lives and loves, and that's the same reason why he was so invested in his students.'

As John and Chaser's star rose, Pilley, an award-winning pianist, singer and composer, used her experience in the music industry to become their manager and producer, as well as Chaser's co-trainer. At the time of John's death they were writing a second book about Chaser together, which she is now working to finish.

She is also the director of a new non-profit called The Chaser Initiative, which will run education programs for young people based on John's techniques and philosophies of fun, individualised, lifelong learning and humans' connection with nature.

'I never imagined I would be using all these tools to manage an old man and his dog at that stage of my life, but it has been an incredible and interesting ride. What I've become is an expert on Chaser and my dad's methods,' she says. 'I've been integrated into this magical community.'

After his death, John's family was touched by the outpouring of support from former students sharing what a profound impact he'd had on their lives. 'We've had hundreds of letters. People reaching out to us, saying, "Dr Pilley changed my life." He was adept at listening to people and encouraging students to follow their bliss and do what makes them happy,' Pilley says. 'He was the ultimate teacher.'

And what about Chaser? How did she cope with saying goodbye to John, the man she loved most in the world, the man who taught her to 'talk'?

Unsurprisingly, many people were very worried about how John's passing would affect his protégé and study buddy, but Pilley says she wasn't one of them. While Chaser spent most of her time with John, she was in every sense a family dog, so she was still surrounded by love and attention after he died. Pilley knew Chaser would be fine – and she was.

Chaser was fourteen when John died, and the effects of age were starting to become more noticeable. She was gradually going deaf, but ever the smartypants, she relied on signed cues and adapted her language skills to become closely attuned to people's body language. 'If she couldn't hear everything immediately, but she was watching us, she would still execute what we were asking. She understood that we were communicating and she was connecting the dots,' says Pilley.

Chaser developed arthritis in her hips, but she never lost her playful spirit and always knew how to get her point across. 'As she got older it was harder for her, but her love of play never diminished and she always had a toy in her mouth.' Pilley laughs. 'If she brought one toy and I didn't respond she'd go get another toy. If I didn't pay attention, she'd move the toy closer, like by my toe or into my lap, and then if I still didn't respond she would actually throw it in my face. Usually that worked, but sometimes she would actually get up in my lap!'

On 23 July 2019, just over a year after John died, Chaser passed away at home and, as Pilley puts it, 'joined John for their next adventure'.

Though she was a stately fifteen years old, Chaser's death still came as a shock to the family. Up until a week before she passed, Chaser was still as energetic and mischievous as ever.

'She was playing with the neighbours' dog, having fun, and she just went downhill very quickly. The vet determined that possibly there was a brain tumour, but we don't really know what happened,' Pilley says. 'I had conversations about donating her brain to science, but at the end of the day she was a member of our family and we couldn't bring ourselves to do it.'

Instead, Chaser was buried in the backyard, alongside Yasha and all the other dogs that John and the Pilley family have loved over the years. Sally, Robin and Pilley held a candlelight vigil and scattered John's ashes with his beloved canine companions.

While their remarkable partnership has ended, both John and Chaser will always be remembered as scholars, trailblazers and, above all, best friends.

Pilley is comforted by the ongoing interest in Chaser and John's work, as well as her own memories of her wonderful father and his equally wonderful dog.

'My father's role often didn't garner as much attention. For some reason there was this perception that Chaser was the unique one and Dad just happened upon this dog. No, no, no. It was him – he was the man behind the dog,' she says. 'I never got tired of watching the two of them together. When I go through video footage of them it just makes me smile every time.'

Today there is a large mural of Chaser in downtown Spartanburg, and in 2020 a bronze statue of her – by Georgia sculptor Betsy Scott – was unveiled at the Children's Museum of the Upstate, also in Spartanburg.

Just as moving are the letters from people whom John and Chaser inspired to teach their own dogs. 'People continue to reach out about Chaser. There are people that are doing things with their own dogs, and that was my father's goal: to talk about these methods and take them even further,' says Pilley. 'It's not going to take more than 1000 toys with your own dog. You just have to get to the point where the dog realises, *Aha! I get it!* And, at the same time, tremendous bonding occurs.'

It's not lost on Pilley that much of John and Chaser's fame – beyond the worlds of academia and canine cognition research – came when Chaser was already an old dog. If proof was needed that age is no barrier to learning, for dogs or any other creature, Chaser is surely it.

'I think what's interesting about dogs is that they have these old souls and this connection, but their spirit always remains willing and childlike and magical. They're unicorns, because they have these unique abilities,' she says. 'They just get better with age. They take care of us and we have to take care of them.'

Chilli

The dog who became a star

It's a common complaint among Hollywood's leading ladies and men that getting older means having fewer juicy roles to choose from. Start showing any visible signs of ageing and the plum parts dry up. A-list heartthrobs suddenly find themselves cast as villains, while silver-screen goddesses are relegated to playing the mothers of the next generation of starlets.

For some actors, however, achieving senior status can be a boon to their careers. These performers only improve with the advent of grey hair and more frequent naps. In some cases, ageing can even lead to the role of a lifetime.

That was the case for Chilli the border collie. He was already well into middle age when he landed a starring role in a major television series. By the time the show concluded, Chilli was twelve – an elderly gentleman by any measure – and had become one of its most beloved characters and cast members.

But while he may have been a late bloomer in TV terms, Chilli always seemed destined for a career in front of an audience. He made his first television appearance when he was just twelve weeks old, and was also a competitive obedience titleholder.

Chilli didn't get a big break so much as follow the path paved by his predecessors: the pack of equally brilliant border collies owned and trained over the years by his owner, Vicki Austin.

Along with her husband, Steve, Vicki is one of Australia's best-known dog trainers. They work with everyday dog owners as well as training dogs for detection and conservation roles such as sniffing out rare and endangered animals. Vicki has even trained quarantine detection dogs for the government of New Caledonia, as well as Tasmania and Western Australia. The couple also provides four-legged talent – both their own dogs and pets belonging to others – for film and television productions.

Vicki's love of dogs started early. Corgis owned by both her parents and grandparents during her childhood taught her formative lessons about unconditional love.

'My parents' corgi, Pepe, was my mate. He was the family pet, but I think I leaned towards him more than my siblings. He was my everything,' she says. 'I can remember, even as a toddler, being in tears or upset with my parents or something, and I understood that dogs were my emotional support. It was always a dog that I turned to when I was excited, happy or sad.'

Vicki was in her late teens when Pepe passed away in 1984 at the stately age of sixteen, and his death devastated the entire family. Vicki's father vowed never to have another dog: he was on the verge of retirement and wanted neither the commitment nor the heartache of losing another much-loved pet.

But Vicki, who was working full-time at a bank but still living at home, desperately missed having a canine companion. 'After six months I approached Dad and said, "Please can I get a dog? I promise I'll look after it."'

She was prepared to plead her case, but to her surprise her father immediately said yes. 'I think he'd been missing having a dog as much as I had.'

Vicki and her boyfriend, who would later become her first husband, decided the dog would be theirs, though it would live with Vicki until they married. Trouble was, the young couple couldn't agree on which breed they wanted.

'I wanted a German shepherd but he'd been chased by one as a child and didn't like them,' she says. 'A little while later we both had a week off work and happened to be watching the kids' TV show *Simon Townsend's Wonder World!* There was a guy that came on with a border collie and it did all sorts of tricks, and that was what inspired us to get one.'

It was love at first sight for Vicki. She knew instantly that the playful, fiercely intelligent border collie was the breed for her. (Incredibly, it later proved to be love of a different kind as well: years after her 2007 marriage to Steve, Vicki 'joined the dots' and realised he had been the trainer she'd seen on the TV show that day.)

From the moment she brought home her first border collie, Radik, Vicki knew life would never be the same. Plenty of dog owners describe their pet as their constant companion, but for Vicki and her then husband it was absolutely true. 'He was like a child. We took him everywhere with us and every minute that we were home he was with us, too.' She laughs. 'It got to the point that our friends just assumed that if they were inviting us somewhere, they were also inviting Radik. People thought we were quite insane.'

Radik led Vicki to her true vocation: dog training. It was something that had never really crossed her mind before. It was the mid-eighties, an era where many family dogs spent the majority of their time alone in the backyard. Most dog owners weren't as proactive or responsible as they are now, and Vicki wasn't even aware that dog training clubs existed.

'When we took Radik to the vet for his puppy vaccinations, the vet said, "Border collies need to be busy and they need something to do, so you need to go to your local dog training club,"' she says.

The vet was absolutely right. A working breed through and through, the border collie was developed to herd livestock, especially sheep, in the Scottish Borders region of the United Kingdom. The breed as we know it today originated towards the end of the nineteenth century, with border collies imported to Australia and New Zealand around the same time, and was bred specifically for intelligence, obedience and trainability.

Border collies are widely believed to be the most intelligent dogs in the world; animal behaviour expert Stanley

Coren ranks the breed at number one on his list of the clev-
erest canines. What that means for modern day working
border collies is that they're extremely motivated to get the
job done.

In a home, however, that innate drive can be problematic. Without proper training and stimulation, it often leads
to destruction. A bored border collie left without a job to
occupy his quick mind will invariably invent one for himself,
and chances are it's not going to be one his owner
appreciates.

So Vicki duly presented herself and Radik at the Hornsby
Dog Training Club on Sydney's upper north shore – and
found her second home.

'We rocked up there and I absolutely loved it and it went
from there,' she says. 'I competed in obedience trials and
won titles with Radik, and later with my other dogs.
I became an instructor and got very heavily involved with
the club on a volunteer basis. It's a really great way to learn
your skills and cut your teeth.'

She went on to become president of the club. The
position brought with it a requirement to make speeches,
run committee meetings and address large groups – a
prospect that terrified Vicki, who was 'an incredibly shy
child and younger person'.

'I was trying – I wanted to do it – but boy, I struggled.
There was no way I could do public speaking,' she says. 'So
off I went to Toastmasters to do a communication course
and, over time, I became more and more confident.' She
couldn't have known the extent to which that training

would come in handy once she became a high-profile professional dog trainer.

Vicki adored obedience training with Radik, especially the deep bond it allowed her to forge with him, and in 1993 she started to wonder whether working with dogs could be a viable career. She had just welcomed her first child, her daughter Lauren, and was on maternity leave from her bank job. It seemed like as good a time as any to test the waters.

'There were very few professional dog trainers back then, and there were no courses I could take to learn, but I'd had a couple of people ask me to help them with their dogs and it crossed my mind that maybe I could make a small income for myself,' she says.

Before long, Vicki was inundated with bookings from dog owners desperate for help with their recalcitrant pets. She was so overwhelmed that she decided to double her price. 'I *still* couldn't manage all the work, so I doubled the price again. I just kept doubling the price until it slowed down to a manageable level,' says Vicki. 'Then I started a puppy school class on my back deck and away I went. I never could have anticipated it.'

As Vicki's career gained momentum, the dog that had inspired it grew older. Vicki continued to train and compete with Radik until he passed away from lung cancer at the age of fourteen. Though grief-stricken by his passing, Vicki was grateful to have had the chance to prepare herself to say goodbye to her best friend.

Tragically, she would not get that opportunity with her next border collie, Kane.

Kane was an Australian obedience champion and the apple of Vicki's eye. He was so successful in the trial ring that he had sired several litters for breeders who wanted their puppies to inherit even a fraction of his intelligence.

But Vicki believes it was that same virility that led to his untimely death in 1995 at the age of eleven. Kane somehow managed to finagle his way out of her property – perhaps on the prowl for more lady friends – and was hit by a car.

His shocking loss left Vicki completely inconsolable. Research shows that symptoms of acute grief after the loss of a pet can persist for a year or more. As a society we don't recognise how painful that can be, or the toll it can take on our mental and physical health.

'It sent me to bed, sobbing, for a week. Kane was the one that really broke my heart. It was an awful time in my life,' Vicki says.

It is testament to Vicki's love for her dogs that her daughter, Lauren, who was a preschooler at the time, was as affected by her mum's anguish as by the loss of Kane, who had been a favourite playmate.

'I got a report from her preschool teacher that Lauren had taken to saying she had a sore tummy and going to lie down. We visited doctors and tried all sorts of things to see if there was anything wrong with her, and nothing could be found,' she says.

The teacher mentioned Lauren's distress to a friend of Vicki's whose child attended the same preschool, explaining that the little girl often talked about 'her mum's old dog'.

'The teacher assumed it was a dog I'd had before Lauren was born. My friend said, "No, she just lost the dog, and she's heartbroken." The teacher suggested I talk to Lauren about Kane,' says Vicki. 'When I did, the floodgates opened.'

Lauren explained to her mum how much she loved Kane and missed him, how she loved playing ball with him. Vicki remembered how soothing the presence of dogs had been for her as a child, and it was clear Lauren felt the same way.

The conversation confirmed for Vicki something she had always felt deep down: she never wanted to be without a dog. As painful as it is to lose a canine companion, she knew then – and still knows – that what we gain from loving dogs is worth the eventual heartache.

'Every time you lose one you think, *Can I go through this again?* But I think I've always known there would always be more dogs,' she says. 'I really do feel sad for kids that grow up without dogs. I feel they miss out on a lot.'

Vicki wasn't left dogless when Kane died: she still had his son, Bodhi, who was then about a year old and already showing great potential on the training front. But she found it difficult to connect with him after losing his dad in the manner she did.

She felt guilty focusing her attention on Bodhi so soon after Kane's death, as though she were casually replacing a dog that had meant so much to her and died well before his time. As a result, she found herself feeling quite distant from the young border collie.

'I went through a period of time where I was keeping Bodhi at arm's length, which was totally unfair,' Vicki says.

'Not too long after, I got a good kick up the backside from an older, experienced dog judge, who said, "If you're not going to love and work with this dog I think you should give it up." I realised then that I did love Bodhi and didn't want anyone else to take him.'

And so Bodhi become a beloved pet and, true to his lineage, a great success in obedience trials. He also went on to train and work in narcotics detection, media and public demonstrations. At the same time, Vicki's dog training career was going from strength to strength, and she was by now also an obedience judge.

Vicki had built such a reputation for excellence in a growing industry that she was soon headhunted for an entirely different type of training. In 2001 she joined Sydney's iconic Taronga Zoo as a trainer and presenter of its Free Flight Bird Show. She spent three years at the zoo, and worked as a consultant trainer to the zoo's Backyard to Bush and marine mammals division for some time, before returning full-time to the dog world.

'I've been very lucky with my business. If I have other things going on and I want to slow it down, I can, and then pick it up when I want to,' she says. Three years after leaving the zoo, she married Steve, who is also a sought-after trainer working primarily with detection and conservation dogs.

Bodhi was getting older and Vicki was starting to think about finding another puppy to start training. Trouble was, after sharing her entire life with such exceptional dogs,

Vicki had exceptionally high standards to meet. She couldn't find an adult dog that felt like the 'right' progenitor for a puppy. 'I like to have my second border collie around when the existing one is five to eight years old. I'd been looking and looking and I just wasn't sold on any particular dog that I would have liked a puppy from.'

But then Steve met a dog that he thought fit the bill. She belonged to a border collie breeder from a rural town near Geelong in Victoria, and she was expecting a litter. 'Steve said, "She's just the most beautiful natured dog, I'm sure you'd like a puppy." I trusted his call,' says Vicki.

Steve was right. When the litter of three girls and four boys was three weeks old, the Austins went to meet the puppies. 'On the way down I was saying, "If this mother's not as perfect as you say she is . . . If this, if that." Of course we got there and the mother was just gorgeous; a superb little dog,' she says. 'She was so lovely with the puppies.'

One puppy in particular caught Vicki's eye, a male with traditional markings. 'I cuddled him and I think we started bonding at that time. He would still be with mum for a few more weeks — his eyes were just starting to open.' She knew immediately that he was the one for her.

Vicki decided to name her new little bundle of fluff Chilli.

As it turned out, hers wasn't the only heart Chilli would steal in his lifetime. More than one million Australian television viewers would soon fall head over heels for him, too.

*

Some trainers maintain a sort of professional detachment from their dogs. Vicki is unapologetically not one of them. Ask her to describe Chilli's temperament and she is unequivocal: 'He's only the best dog that's ever walked the earth.'

Virtually from the moment she brought him home, Chilli has shown himself to be the gentlest of souls. He adores people and loves other dogs, and he possesses an uncanny ability to calm any situation. 'I often say that Chilli has a PhD in social skills and communication, both with dogs and people. I've never seen anything like him in a dog before,' says Vicki. 'He's so intuitive with people. If somebody is fearful or uncomfortable, he doesn't rush them. He takes his time. He'll sidle up to them and eventually get them to pat him.'

Vicki offers consultations to dog owners whose pets have behavioural issues such as phobias or aggression, and she often brings Chilli with her to these appointments. He has proven to be an excellent role model for dogs in need of guidance. 'He's absolutely phenomenal. He just takes the social pressure of other dogs and they can relax in his company. It's Chilli that gives them the grounding in how to handle themselves.'

While she jokes that she's more than willing to take the credit for his angelic nature, Vicki concedes that Chilli was simply born this way.

'I always said with all my previous border collies that, in the wrong home, they could have been problematic. But Chilli could have gone into any home and just been a lovely dog,' she says. 'That's just the way he is naturally.'

Chilli was no stranger to the spotlight, either. He took part in his first film shoot when he was just twelve weeks old, posing with popular TV vet Dr Harry Cooper in a segment about puppy training on the popular *Better Homes & Gardens* television show. He continued to appear regularly on the show after that. But Vicki never actively tried to promote Chilli as a performer, preferring to work with him in her training classes and private consultations.

But in 2012, the producers of a new television series got in touch with Steve. They wanted to cast a working breed pooch that could play a farm dog in fifties Australia. Steve, who works with the media more often than Vicki, knew Chilli and his easygoing approach to life would be perfect in the role.

The show was *A Place to Call Home*, created by Bevan Lee, the man who brought such legendary series as *Sons and Daughters, All Saints* and *Packed to the Rafters* to Australian television screens. Set in rural NSW after World War II, it follows Sarah Adams as she returns to Australia to start a new life after twenty years abroad. The producers asked Steve to find a dog to play the companion of kindly old farmer Roy Briggs, played by veteran actor Frankie J Holden, who takes Sarah under his wing.

'Life is always so much easier if you can work with your own dog in media jobs, so Steve and I convinced them Chilli was the dog for the job,' says Vicki. 'Certainly border collies were around in Australia in the fifties, though they would not have been as pretty as Chilli. We said he was very trainable and adaptable, and they decided to go with him.'

There was one condition to Chilli's employment as Roy's dog, Lucky: he had to look a little rougher around the edges.

'Initially they said, "He has to look like a rough old abandoned farm dog, so we'll have to make him look less pretty and muddy him up a bit." Basically, he would go into make-up before the scene he was shooting and they would coat him with mud. It was quite funny to see him looking so dirty and scruffy.'

But making a dog as gorgeous as Chilli look down-trodden was laborious work, and the producers eventually decided to let his natural beauty shine through. 'It wasn't long into the series that they just gave up on the mud. Originally his character was this unloved, abandoned farm dog, but later he was loved so they decided he could be pretty.'

A Place to Call Home debuted on Channel Seven in April 2013 and soon became Australia's top-rating drama, drawing an average audience of 1.47 million. Its second season averaged a still respectable 800,000 viewers, but halfway through the run Seven announced it would not renew the show for a third season.

The backlash was swift and fierce. The network, it seemed, had underestimated the passion of the show's legions of fans, who were outraged by the decision to axe the series. A barrage of online petitions begging Seven to save the show attracted thousands of signatures, while the 'Save A Place to Call Home' Facebook group soon had more than 6000 members.

Seven stood firm on its decision, but at the eleventh hour pay-TV network Foxtel threw the show a lifeline, picking it up for a third season. *A Place to Call Home* ran for six seasons in all, and Chilli starred in every single one.

'I was absolutely floored. Chilli had his own little fan club. They just went mad, it was crazy stuff,' says Vicki. 'But it was because of those people that Foxtel picked up the show and ran with it.'

Chilli, by now six years old, took to his new career like a duck to water. He was doted on by the entire cast and crew. 'He just loved being on set and the people loved him. Everybody paid him a lot of attention. I remember one person saying to me, "When you turn up to work and Chilli's here you know it's going to be a good day."'

Actress Marta Dusseldorp, who played Sarah Adams, described her canine co-star as loyal, smart and patient. 'Chilli is an absolute charmer with the softest eyes in the business,' she told *Dogs Life* magazine in 2014. 'Sarah and Lucky were instant soulmates. Chilli and I also bonded easily, especially as Vicki gave me dog treats to keep in my hand before the take.'

Chilli did have the occasional cheeky moment, however. In the show's first season, he had to film a scene in which Sarah tries to leave town and Lucky follows her.

'She gets off her bike and picks up a rock to throw at him to make him go away. Chilli thought it was a game and went chasing the rock,' Vicki recalls. (The 'rock' was made of foam and would not have hurt Chilli, even if it had hit him.)

Such was Chilli's determination to fetch the rock, the

scene eventually had to be filmed in two parts. 'You saw Marta pick up the rock and go to throw it and then they cut it. They filmed Chilli separately, looking like he was chasing after Marta, and I've made him cringe to make it seem as though the rock was being thrown.'

In the same episode, Lucky is accidentally hit by Roy's truck. That emotional scene was created a little differently to how it appeared on screen, too.

'In distress, Sarah picks him up. But Chilli weighs 22 kilograms and Marta's not a big woman,' says Vicki. 'When they called "action" I would pick him up and put him in her arms, then I'd be just off camera, ready to catch him because she couldn't hold him for too long.'

The scene really allowed Chilli to show off his acting chops. It aired on Mother's Day 2014 and Vicki was at her sister's house, watching the show with their mother. 'When Lucky got hit by the truck I turned around and there was my mum with tears streaming down her face,' she says. 'I said, "Mum, he's fine. He's right here at your feet!" She said, "He's just such a good actor."'

Of course, Chilli didn't understand that he was acting. For the duration of his time on the show, he very much felt that he belonged to Marta and Frankie J Holden, sticking to the pair like glue. 'He very much caught on to the fact that Lucky's people in the show were *his* people. They didn't need to have him on a lead. Chilli knew that his role was to be around either Frankie or Marta,' she says. 'It got to the point that if they got up to move off set he would go with them. In his mind he was their dog.'

By 2018, during filming of the final season of *A Place to Call Home*, Chilli was twelve. While his age was beginning to catch up with him, he remained dedicated to his role.

'In the early seasons, Chilli could jump up onto the back of Roy's truck. But as the years went on he did less and less jumping,' says Vicki. 'Although he wasn't as nimble as in his earlier years, he was still "Roy's dog" and would follow him wherever he went, looking very natural.'

Chilli was also becoming hard of hearing, and today is almost completely deaf, so the timing of the show's end proved fortuitous. 'Had that happened while we were still shooting, it would have been problematic. It was very lucky the series finished when it did.'

Towards the end of the show, Chilli was diagnosed with kidney disease. He was eleven at the time and the onset of the illness was sudden and shocking.

'It was very clear: out of the blue he started drinking a lot more water. It came on very strong,' Vicki says. 'It was panic stations at first when the vet took his blood pressure and said, "Without medication he's at death's door."' Thankfully, that medication brought the symptoms of the disease under control. Chilli now has quarterly blood tests to monitor the condition, which currently isn't causing him too much trouble.

He went on to star in another Foxtel series, *Fighting Season,* which aired in 2018, and then stepped out of the spotlight. Although he did briefly return to the small screen in 2020, playing a minor role in the Network Ten drama series *The Secrets She Keeps*. Chilli is now enjoying his well-earned retirement while Vicki works on training her younger border collie, Lisa. Vicki and Steve have six dogs between them: Chilli, Lisa, Steve's pet German shepherd Django, plus two English springer spaniels and a cocker spaniel that he uses as conservation detection dogs. (Steve also used Chilli for many years in his Assessing and Handling Dangerous Dogs presentations all over Australia.)

Chilli is most definitely the leader of the pack, and Vicki admits he enjoys a few more privileges than his younger counterparts.

While his kidney disease will likely shorten his life to some extent, Chilli is fourteen now and still comfortable and happy – and what a life it's been.

Vicki says caring for a senior dog is a privilege that too many people take for granted. 'You've shared their lifetime, and sadly that life is so much shorter than ours, but you know everything that's gone into that life when you've raised them from a puppy. There's a very good chance that everything that dog knows or has experienced, you have been there,' she says.

'Dogs are the only species that has evolved to prefer the company of humans. That is incredibly special, and yet we take it for granted all the time. I don't think we place enough value on what dogs give us.'

And for those of us who do, there is simply no way to measure that value.

Suzy

The dog who came in from the cold

What's the most unexpected thing you can imagine finding in your house at four o'clock in the morning? A burglar, perhaps? A sheepish teenager sneaking in well after curfew? Maybe a disoriented bird that has fluttered down the chimney, or a creepy crawly that has slithered through a gap under the door? All would certainly be shocking.

But what about a cold, wet and injured senior dog?

That's precisely what Jack and Emily Jokinen discovered in the kitchen of their home in Philadelphia in the wee hours of 14 December 2019.

The stunned couple owned a dog – but not this dog. They had never seen *this* dog before. It hadn't been in the house when they'd gone to bed. And even more astonishingly, all their doors and windows were closed and locked. Which invites the question: *How on earth did it get in?*

First, let's meet the Jokinens. It's important to understand that, while Emily is a devoted and lifelong dog lover, Jack had been a little slower to embrace canine companionship.

'Emily had dogs her whole life and very much wanted a dog when we met. She always talked about getting a dog, then after we got the first dog, she always talked about getting a second dog,' he says. 'When I was very young we had a dog but I felt no connection with it – it was my dad's dog from when he was in his twenties. I never wanted a dog. There was never that longing to have one.'

It wasn't that Jack didn't like dogs. It was simply that, after he finished college and embarked on a career in technology, he was realistic about his primary focus at that point in his life: himself. He knew he couldn't give a dog the sort of life it deserved.

'I viewed having a dog as an obligation. When I first started to see friends getting dogs after college, I was still single. I thought, *If I can go walk a dog at the end of the day or go to happy hour, I'm going to happy hour,*' he explains. 'Having a dog is a commitment – at least, it is if you do it right.'

When they got married in 2015, Jack and Emily were living in New York City – he's a Bronx native, and she had moved there for a job. Home was a small apartment, and they weren't willing to keep a dog cooped up inside all day.

In 2017, however, they decided to move back to Philly, where they had first met (at Drexel University). The cost of living was much lower there, meaning they could afford a house with a yard, and they were still close enough to New York to visit whenever they felt the need.

And Emily could finally get the dog she had been dreaming of, despite Jack's ongoing reluctance.

'I said to her that if we moved back to Philly I would get her a dog for her birthday. My one condition was that it had to be a rescue. That was what felt natural to me,' says Jack.

So they made the move to the riverside neighbourhood of Fishtown, and Emily set about searching online for her perfect pet. She soon found an adorable mixed-breed puppy in the care of a local rescue group called Rescue Dogs Rock.

'She reached out to them, but the dog had already been adopted. But it was part of a litter of puppies who all had red-themed names: Rusty, Brick, Cliff, after the *Clifford the Big Red Dog* kids' books,' Jack says.

Rusty caught Emily's eye, and she and Jack went to meet the pup, who was about six months old. It was love at first sight for his wife, but Jack was still resisting conversion to full 'dog person' status.

'He was a sweet puppy and Emily was like, "This is it, this is what I want." I said, "Okay, we'll come back next week and get the dog." But I really did not want a dog,' he says. 'Even on the way to pick him up I said, "I want to reiterate that I'm doing this because I love you, and I do not want a dog."'

Part of his reticence stemmed from the fact that Jack now worked from home while Emily still went out to work each day. In addition to his day job, he also hosts the popular *George's Box* podcast, which focuses on the New York

Yankees and Major League Baseball generally, as well as a web series called *Stadium Eats*, which reviews food at sports stadiums.

Jack knew that 'their' dog would essentially be *his* dog, and he wasn't sure he was up for that.

But he had made a promise and he was true to his word. Rusty came home to Fishtown. They renamed him Jorge Pawsada, after Yankees catcher Jorge Posada.

'He was down in the basement where my office is. I came down and he looked terrified, and I said, "Hey, I'm scared, too,"' Jack says. 'But working from home was new for me, so I didn't realise how lonely I would be, not going to the office and seeing people every day. He became my best friend.'

His transformation from dog-averse to president of the Jorge appreciation society was so complete that Jack quickly became a passionate advocate of rescue. Jorge even had a starring role in a *Stadium Eats* webisode filmed at the Philadelphia Phillies' annual Bark at the Park event, when dogs are allowed to accompany their owners to a baseball game at the team's home field, Citizens Bank Park.

'After we adopted Jorge, I really got into the idea of always rescuing and never buying a dog,' he says. 'I thought it would be funny to bring Jorge to the event and make a little video saying, "Adopt, adopt, adopt."'

Jorge settled in, and life got even busier for the Jokinens. In November 2019, Emily and Jack welcomed their first child, daughter Johanna Rose, known as Joey. A month later, Jack's parents travelled to Philly from their home in Florida to meet their first grandchild and spend Christmas with the family.

'There was a lot going on, and we were just trying to keep things moving,' says Jack.

And right then, when they really did not need anything more on their plates, a stray senior dog came in from the cold.

Philly winters are notoriously brutal. Heavy rain and howling winds are common, temperatures frequently plummet below freezing, and at least one or two decent snowfalls are to be expected each year.

The night of 13 December 2019 was certainly playing to type. The cold was biting, it was windy, and the rain was coming in sideways. Jack wasn't exactly relishing the prospect of taking Jorge out at nine o'clock at night for a short walk down the street so the little dog could relieve himself before bed. (That he refuses to answer the call of nature in his own backyard is one of Jorge's less endearing quirks).

Jack took him out anyway, because that's what good dog owners do, but it wasn't the most pleasant of strolls for either of them.

'There was a big storm going on. I was in my raincoat and I had my umbrella and the dog,' he recalls. 'Jorge did his thing and we went back inside. I had towels by the door and I dried him off, got my raincoat off. I closed the door and eventually we went to bed.'

73

With a newborn baby in the house, Jack and Emily had become used to broken sleep. But when Emily woke him up at 3.53 a.m. and he opened his bleary eyes to see her standing over him, he knew something was amiss.

'The first thing she said was, "The baby's okay," because she knew that's the first place my mind would go,' he says. 'Then she said, "There's a dog in the house."'

Not yet fully awake, at first Jack thought that Emily was referring to Jorge, who was sleeping at the foot of their bed. 'I said, "Yeah, Jorge. He's right there."'

But Emily was most definitely *not* talking about Jorge. 'She said, "No, there's a puppy in the house and I don't know where it came from."'

Still not fully comprehending the situation, he tried to reassure his wife. Emily had been downstairs to fetch a dummy for baby Joey, and Jack assumed that Jorge had somehow sneaked past her and then returned to his slumber in the couple's bedroom. 'I said, "You're tired, you just had a baby, there's a lot going on."'

But Emily was adamant: there was a four-legged intruder in their home, and Jack needed to do something about it. *Now*.

So Jack got out of bed and went downstairs with Emily in tow. Sure enough: 'There was this wet, injured, terrified puppy, just sitting in the middle of the kitchen.'

He couldn't immediately tell if the dog was male or female, but he could see that the poor creature wasn't in great shape. It was emaciated, with every ridge of its spine showing through its thin fur, and it had a noticeable limp.

'You just had to look at it and you'd think, *This dog is not healthy*,' says Jack.

The couple immediately grabbed a blanket and wrapped up the shivering creature. Then they carried it downstairs to Jack's basement office, where he had a large pen set up for Jorge. They put the dog in the pen with some food so that it would be safe and secure while they figured out what on earth they were going to do next.

Almost without thinking about it, Jack grabbed his phone and snapped a picture of the dog. It looked so forlorn, eyes downcast, bundled up in the blue blanket. A frequent user of Twitter, he tweeted the photo to his 30,000-plus followers, along with the caption, 'I just woke up to this puppy in my house and we have no idea how it got here.'

With the dog out of harm's way, Jack's thoughts turned to how it could possibly have got inside the house. The conclusion he came to was terrifying.

'At that moment I was thinking, *Someone broke into my house*. Someone clearly broke in, and they're hiding,' he says. 'I walked Emily upstairs to the baby and said, "Stay here." Then I got a butcher's knife and started searching the house.'

He checked the front and back doors: both closed and locked up tight. He checked the ground floor windows: also locked. Then he started on the bathrooms and closets.

'I checked the baby's room, and then I realised I had to check my parents' room. I opened the door and said, "Hey, are you alive?" I was standing there with a knife and they're like, "Huh?" I said, "Good, you're alive. I'm just going to check your closet. Go back to sleep."'

Thankfully, yet bafflingly, there was nobody in the house, and there was no sign of forced entry. How, then, had they acquired a soaked and starving dog in the middle of the night?

There was one tool at Jack's disposal that might just help to solve the puzzle: security cameras. Via an app on his phone, he pulled up the footage from the cameras at the front of his property.

'At 3.16 a.m., there's the dog coming down the block, limping. It's raining. The dog stops in front of my house, looks up, and sees that there's a door open,' he says. 'The dog checks it out, goes back and forth, unsure. Eventually it goes in the house, a minute later comes out, then it goes back in.'

Jack continued scrubbing through the footage. All was quiet and still for another fifteen minutes, until the camera picked up a man walking down the street.

'This guy walks by and sees the door open. He goes up to the door and yells and knocks, then pulls the door shut. This was only ten minutes before Emily got up. If the door had still been open she probably would have startled the dog and it would have run out,' says Jack.

(Thanks to the power of the internet, Jack later learned that the good Samaritan was called Steve, and that he was returning home from a night on the town when he noticed the Jokinens' front door wide open. Jack was able to take Steve out for dinner to thank him.)

Now Jack knew that the dog had entered the house through the open front door, no doubt seeking shelter from the awful storm. But *why* had the door been open? Jack distinctly remembered shutting it when he and Jorge returned from their late-evening walk. It just didn't make any sense.

'Our door handle auto-locks after three or four seconds, so I went back even further into the footage, wondering, *How did this door get open?*' he says. 'What had happened was that in my rush to get out of the rain with Jorge I didn't close it all the way and the door didn't catch. Then when the storm got bad, it blew open, and stayed open until Steve came along.'

That answered some questions, then. But there were still so many others. Where had the dog come from? Did it have an owner? Why did it look so sick? And what were they going to do with it? 'It was so injured that my initial thought was, *We just have to get this dog back to where it came from.*'

Emily had some thoughts about the situation. 'My wife said, "I don't want to start a fight, but this is my dog now."' Jack laughs. 'I was saying, "No, it's probably a puppy from around the corner, a Christmas gift. We'll get it checked for a microchip and take it back." I was still half asleep at this point.'

But Jack knew he was too wired to go back to sleep. Instead, he stayed up for the rest of the night, searching for potential solutions to their odd problem.

'I was literally googling "what to do if you find a dog in your house". I looked up animal control. They opened at

8 a.m., so I was on the phone at one minute past saying, "Here's the situation."'

Animal control is the US equivalent of a local council pound, and the staff there were helpful, but the options they presented made Jack feel uncomfortable.

'They said, "Yeah, you can just come and drop it off at 11 a.m. and we'll take care of it." That just didn't feel right. I don't know much about dogs, but that answer wasn't sufficient for me, so we called our vet that opens at nine a.m.

'In the meantime my dad came downstairs, like, "Did you come into our room with a knife?"'

The couple's regular vet clinic was fully booked for the day and not able to see the mystery dog, so the Jokinens kept searching until they found a nearby emergency vet hospital. Staff told them to bring in the dog – which the couple had by now established was a girl – right away.

When the vets checked the weary pup, they found that not only did she not have a microchip, the sad mixed-breed canine was in much worse physical condition than first impressions suggested.

'She had fleas and ticks, she had a heart murmur, she had infections in all four of her paw pads. One of her feet was deformed, so that was making the limp worse,' says Jack. 'She was very malnourished. Her mouth was atrocious and she was going to need a ton of dental work down the road. The vet said they'd work up a cost estimate for us so we could figure out what we wanted to do.'

And the vet had another bombshell: the dog wasn't a puppy at all. She was certainly small, owing to her emaciated condition, but she was actually somewhere between seven and nine years old, officially making her a senior.

There was no doubt that treating a senior dog's laundry list of ailments was going to be expensive. If they took her to a shelter, Jack and Emily wouldn't have to shoulder the burden of those enormous bills.

Then again, if they took her to a shelter, chances were she would be deemed too old and unwell to save.

In the short time she had been with them, the dog seemed to have become attached to Jack. She followed him every-where, even sitting under his chair at the vet hospital. She had been courageous enough to seek and find help in the middle of a raging storm. Could they really bring them-selves to give her up?

'This dog had to have been hours from death when she found our house. The weather was nasty for a few more days,' says Jack. 'Maybe if she hadn't come into our place, she would have been picked up and taken to the pound, but nobody was adopting this dog. Nobody was going to invest what you'd have to invest in this dog.'

Emily, for one, had no doubt about the best course of action. 'She was like, "I get it – we have a one month old, we're trying to get Jorge used to the baby, your parents are here, but . . ."'

But. That one little word meant so much. The funny thing was, Jack felt it too.

'I kept saying to myself, "I hate that I know I'm going to do the right thing here." I remember at some point that morning saying, "There's no other way it goes than we adopt this dog." When the vet came back with the estimate, I didn't even look at it. I just said, "Let's do it – we'll work it out.'"

Just like that, the Jokinens were a two-dog family.

Jack and Emily took their new family member home. On the way, they bought her a collar and decided on a name: Suzyn Pupman, after Suzyn Waldman, the Yankees' radio announcer. She would be Suzy for short.

But if the couple thought this was the end of the crazy tale, they were mistaken. Suzy's story was just beginning.

Amid all the frantic googling, phone calls and trips to the vet, Jack had continued to tweet the saga in real time to an increasingly invested audience. He shared pictures of the dog now known as Suzy at the vet and clips from the security camera footage. The story of the dog that came in from the cold was starting to go viral, with high profile personalities like sports analyst and podcaster Pat McAfee sharing Jack's tweets.

Before he knew what was happening, complete strangers were reaching out to Jack via Twitter with offers of support. People pledged to adopt Suzy if Jack and Emily decided not to keep her, while others wanted to contribute to covering her veterinary costs.

Once the couple had agreed she was staying, Jack shared the news with Suzy's new legion of fans. 'I posted a quick video where I just kind of summarised what had happened.

I threw in at the end, "Here's my Venmo [a payment app] details, but if no one gives a penny this dog will be okay, we'll take care of her.'"

Incredibly, over the next two months, more than US$40,000 was donated. If Jack and Emily had been surprised to find a stray dog in their kitchen, they were absolutely blown away by the generosity of strangers.

'We never asked for money. I never pushed it. But especially here in America, things aren't that great; there's a tension,' he says. 'So maybe people needed something to believe in.'

When Jack and Emily got Suzy home that first day, they hoped for some quiet time to help their new pet settle in, as well as to introduce her to both Jorge and Joey – not to mention for the two of them to catch up on some sleep.

They didn't get it.

Local TV news channel FOX 29 had got wind of the story and asked Jack if they could write about it for their blog.

'This was Saturday morning, and the blog went out on Saturday night. On Sunday I was on NBC, Fox, CBS, ABC, *Inside Edition*. Suzy was on the cover of the *Philadelphia Daily News*. Then the *Washington Post* picked it up. The animal website *The Dodo* did a video that, the last time I checked, has had more than 40 million views,' he says.

'We just started seeing it everywhere. All of a sudden, everybody and their mum knew about it. I spent the first week just doing interviews nonstop. My parents were here for a week, and I hardly saw them.'

Emily already ran a fun Instagram account for Jorge (@jorge_pawsada) and they decided to set one up for Suzy as well. Before long @suzynpupman had 46,000 followers eager for regular updates on her progress with the Jokinens.

The couple figured Suzymania would die down before long, but the media requests, messages of support and unsolicited donations just kept coming. Suzy was frequently recognised in public and Jack started being approached by people who wanted to know if he was 'Suzy's dad'. She even has her own post-office box, which is regularly flooded with letters and gifts.

'She had to have an echocardiogram to see if she was fit to go under anaesthetic for her dental work. The nurse came in to get some background, and I said that we'd just sort of found her. I didn't say, "She's a famous dog." Then they go out the back and I hear yelling. The nurse comes back, like, "Is this . . . Suzy?" It was crazy.'

Even with all the attention, Jack didn't fully understand just how far Suzy's story had spread. Not until a good friend who had relocated to London shared an anecdote. Jack's friend and his wife were having lunch with a friend, a Frenchman who worked as a translator. Also at the lunch was the translator's client, a wealthy Japanese woman.

Jack's friend began to tell the story of how his pal back in Philly had found a dog in his house in the middle of the night. The translator was retelling the story in Japanese when his client motioned for him to stop. She leaned closer and said, 'Everyone in Japan knows Suzy.'

Then the adoptions began. Jack and Emily started receiving messages from people all over the US, Canada and even the UK who'd been so touched by Suzy's incredible tale of rescue that they had gone out and adopted pets themselves, many of them senior dogs, just like Suzy.

'We've been trying to encourage people to adopt, and celebrate the people who do,' he says. Jack started sharing each adoption on Suzy's Instagram account, highlighting the good that can come from giving an animal a second chance. Within six months, he had shared seventy-five adoption stories that had been directly inspired by Suzy.

As the Suzy juggernaut rolled on, Jack spent a lot of time researching other 'internet famous' dogs. He and Emily knew they wanted to use Suzy's celebrity status – and the money donated in her name – to have a wider impact.

'We said, "We don't want $40,000." I mean, we wouldn't turn it down if someone said, "Here, have $40,000 just for you," but it was given to us for dogs,' says Jack. 'I started looking at what famous dogs do, what they stand for and what they get behind. We wanted to make sure Suzy is okay and then we wanted to start donating the money. The goal is to give away all the money.'

They decided to start by sponsoring 100 adoptions of senior pets, to the tune of US$10,000. After that, who knows? Jack has plenty of ideas, but for now he's just rolling with the punches. He maintains a publicly accessible spreadsheet of every donation received and every dollar spent.

Away from the spotlight, Suzy is continuing to thrive. She has gained weight, her paw infections have healed, and her heart murmur is under control and doesn't yet require medication. She had seventeen rotten teeth removed and is now much more comfortable.

Jack and Emily weren't able to find out anything about Suzy's past life, and nobody ever came forward to claim her, but they suspect she was somebody's pet at some point. She seemed to understand basic obedience commands from the start, and she adores baby Joey, which made the couple wonder if she had lived with children before.

Jorge was surprisingly accepting of his new canine sibling, and after some initial growly hesitancy from Suzy – 'She was a tough street dog,' says Jack – the two now get on like a house on fire.

Jack, however, remains the apple of Suzy's eye – and not always in a healthy way. She follows him everywhere and frets whenever he's out of sight.

One night she and Jorge were barred from the bedroom after Jack had knee surgery and couldn't risk the dogs jumping on him. Suzy expressed her displeasure by barking all night and destroying everything within chewing distance.

On another occasion, her separation anxiety revealed itself in particularly gruesome fashion.

'I put her in her crate while I took Joey to visit my in-laws, just for a couple of hours. When we got back I walked in the house and I was like, "There is a smell in this house that I've never smelled before." It was pee, it was poop, and it was blood,' Jack says. 'She had flipped her water bowl and busted one of her nails and she was just covered in blood. It was all over her.'

Jack and Emily are now exploring different options for treating Suzy's anxiety.

Jack shared the frightening experience with Suzy's Instagram family. It was the first time they had posted anything that could be construed as negative and they were curious what her fans' reaction would be.

'This is a senior street dog and there are drawbacks. Suzy is a sweet dog, but I'm not going to sugar-coat it,' he says. 'Everyone was very supportive, and it was a good reality check. If you adopt a dog, it's not necessarily going to be easy.'

Jack and Emily can't help but marvel at how much, and how quickly, their lives changed because that senior street dog saw an open door on a stormy night and decided to make the most of it.

Jack doesn't think there was anything fated or magical about Suzy choosing his house to shelter in that night. Rather, he puts it down to her pluck, her street smarts and her survival instinct. 'I left a door open because I was tired and I have a baby. The house was light and warm and probably smelled like dog and food.'

Whether it was her sense of self-preservation or something else that led Suzy to step through that door, Jack is certainly glad she did. She has given thousands of people so much joy, saved the lives of other dogs through adoption, and shown everybody who encounters her that senior dogs are worthy of love and care.

'It's an incredible story and an incredible honour. We're grateful for this opportunity to do something positive, to show that there are good people in the world and that you can make a difference,' says Jack.

'I believe everyone has an interesting story to tell and this is part of our interesting story. For some people it's the most interesting part and, if that helps save some dog and cat lives, that's great.'

From being unsure he would ever want a dog to welcoming first Jorge and then Suzy, and becoming a staunch advocate of rescue and adoption, the experience has also given Jack a renewed sense of purpose.

'Everything in my life was good. I had a wife, a great job, a nice new house. But I didn't realise I was depressed. Then I got Jorge, and it all changed,' he says. 'If one of these adoptions is that person's Jorge or Suzy, that's awesome.'

That's the thing: you don't need to find a sick old dog in your kitchen in the middle of the night to find your best friend. All you have to do is visit a shelter and open your heart.

Maya

The dog who saves koalas

In the southern hemisphere summer of 2019–20, most of Australia was on fire. The bushfire season, which usually begins in October on the country's eastern seaboard, started months ahead of schedule in response to devastating drought and several serious fires that broke out as early as June.

The horror season, which came to be known as the Black Summer, saw hundreds of fires burning for weeks on end, mainly in Australia's south-east. Firefighters, supplies and equipment were shipped in from countries including Canada, New Zealand, Singapore and the United States, and the Australian Defence Force was mobilised to provide additional manpower and logistical support.

By March 2020, the fires had burnt through more than 18 million hectares, or 186,000 square kilometres. They destroyed nearly 6000 buildings, including 2779 homes, and claimed the lives of at least thirty-four people.

The infernos are believed to have killed around a billion animals, driving some species to the brink of extinction. The iconic koala was one of the worst hit species, with experts estimating up to 10,000 may have perished in the blazes, including 5000 in New South Wales alone.

It was a bleak beginning to a year that went on to be one of the most challenging in living memory. The devastating losses dismayed scientists working to protect koala populations in NSW and Queensland, which were already under pressure as a result of land clearing, climate change and domestic animal attacks.

Koalas reproduce in a decidedly leisurely fashion, with each female able to give birth to only one joey per year, so repopulation after the fires would be agonisingly slow. That was why it was important for ecologists to know precisely how many were still out there in the scorched bush – or as precisely as the notoriously shy animals would allow. And of course it was vital that they find any sick or injured koalas quickly, so they could receive potentially lifesaving veterinary treatment.

That's where Bear came in. A five-year-old rescued koolie, Bear is part of the Detection Dogs for Conservation program at the University of the Sunshine Coast in Queensland. He is trained to find both koalas and quolls (another small marsupial) in their natural habitat.

In the midst of the Black Summer, Bear was deployed to sniff out injured koalas in fire-ravaged areas. Pictures of him doing exactly that promptly went viral. The protective-bootie-clad 'hero koala dog' was splashed across screens and front pages across Asia, Europe and the USA.

But, as wonderful as he is, this story isn't about Bear. A wise person once quipped that 'behind every successful man stands a strong woman,' and that is true of Bear. He wouldn't have found international fame if not for the *two* fearless females who paved the way: Romane Cristescu and her senior dog, Maya.

This story is about them.

Growing up, Romane was something of a frustrated dog lover. She would have loved to have a dog, but her parents vetoed the idea, so instead she had anything else they would allow. Her childhood menagerie included guinea pigs, hamsters, rabbits, mice, fish, turtles, parrots and even a mole. She was especially fond of cats and always had at least one feline friend. She loved wildlife, too. Or rather, her scientist's brain was fascinated by native animals, their habits and habitat.

After initially training as a vet in her native France, Romane shifted gears and became an ecologist, studying the relationships between organisms and their environments. She moved to Australia in 2007 to complete PhD research into koalas in human-made habitats. (Man-made or reha-bilitated habitats, such as tree plantations established after mining, are those that have been created or manipulated by humans in an effort to mimic a natural environment.)

The tricky thing about studying koalas is that they are hard to find: they camouflage remarkably well against the grey-green leaves of their preferred eucalyptus trees.

And their voracious appetites mean they move around a lot; adult koalas eat up to a kilogram of leaves every day, so they regularly change tree.

Consequently, the easiest way for ecologists to identify koala habitats is not by looking for actual koalas but for koala scat, which is the scientific term for poo.

'Wildlife doesn't want to be found. Their survival instinct is to hide from you. Koalas are really cryptic and low density, so if you're trying to find where they live by looking for koalas, you're going to spend a lot of days searching for them with little result,' Romane explains. 'But Koalas poo eighty to one hundred times a day, and those scats can stay in the environment for many months or even years, so you've got a lot more chance of finding a koala poo than a koala.'

The poo is akin to a koala guidebook, revealing a wealth of valuable information about the animals. DNA can be extracted from the scat, which allows scientists to study the level of genetic diversity and inbreeding in the population – known as gene flow – as well as disease-causing pathogens and genetic fingerprinting.

'Gene flow means how connected to or isolated from each other they are. We want to see connectivity, but it's something that humans tend to break when we build roads or towns, and in agricultural landscapes,' she says. 'If koalas are geographically isolated, they're going to have no choice but to breed with relatives. The more genetic diversity they have, the more tools they have against anything we, or the environment, can throw at them. In the long term they will be able to cope with more things.'

Unfortunately, locating small, round, brown koala droppings on the ground among a lot of thick, equally brown leaf litter is pretty difficult, too. As Romane carried out the laborious task day after day, she got to thinking there had to be a better way.

'I had great big areas of land to cover and I was on my own, looking for little brown pellets. It was quite boring, after months of doing that on my hands and knees, but it allowed me a lot of time to think,' she says. 'I started thinking that maybe there was another animal that could find these scats by relying on their nose.

'Koala poo is very smelly, but it doesn't smell like poo – it smells like eucalyptus. Using your eyes, they are quite hard to spot, but for dogs the smell would be like a rose in the bush.'

Dogs weren't in common use for conservation work at this stage. In fact, Romane didn't even know conservation dogs existed in Australia – she describes her feeling that canines might be well suited to the job as 'just a hunch'.

She contacted several professional dog trainers to discuss her idea. It's something of an understatement to say none was particularly enthused.

'They all thought I was an idiot,' says Romane.

Discouraged by the response, she set the idea aside while she completed her PhD. By 2012, she had earned her doctorate and was officially Dr Cristescu. Jobs in both ecology and academia are hard to come by, however, and she hadn't managed to secure employment. She wasn't even sure she would stay in Australia.

She definitely was *not* in the ideal position to take on a rescue dog.

But dogs don't care about that, do they?

Through a mutual acquaintance, Romane happened to meet a dog trainer by the name of Gary 'Gaz' Jackson. She mentioned to him that she had once hoped to train a dog to detect koala scat, but the plan had been scuppered by dubious members of his own profession.

'He looked at me and said, "But that's so easy!"' she recalls. Gaz fell in love with the idea of helping her to train a koala detection dog. 'I said, "I don't even know if I'm going to stay in the country! Should I get a dog if I'm going to leave in a month?"'

But her new friend was excited by the project, though he was a little put off by the idea of training a dog to find poo. Wouldn't finding the animals themselves be a little more pleasant?

'I told him I didn't need the animal, I needed the poo. Gaz said, "It's not glamorous." And I said, "*I'm* not glamorous – I'm an ecologist and I need the poo!"' She laughs.

After a robust discussion, Gaz agreed to help Romane locate a suitable dog and train it to find koala scat. A few weeks later, he called to say he'd found her. 'He said, "I have your dog." I was like, *I have no job! I don't even know where I'm going to live!*'

Nevertheless, curiosity compelled her to meet this dog who Gaz was so sure would make a great scat detector. He had found her at a local shelter – Romane believes her former owners simply abandoned her outside, leaving no name and no history. She decided to call her Mayamaya, which she had discovered means 'dog' in the Pitta Pitta language once spoken in what is now western Queensland; she would be Maya for short.

'My understanding is that she was supposed to be put down on the day Gaz rescued her, but the vet nurse at the clinic didn't want to put her down,' she says.

The nurse's reluctance may have had something to do with the fact that Maya was only a young dog; she estimated her age to be somewhere between one and four.

But despite her youth, Maya wasn't in great shape. 'She was a very smelly ball of fluff, and she was really scared,' says Romane. 'She had very bad wear on her teeth, I think probably from eating and chasing stones.'

Under all the grime, however, Romane could see that Maya was a very pretty dog. She gave her a thorough wash and took her to the beach, where she was convinced Maya had her first glimpse of the ocean. 'I'm sure she had never seen the sea. She didn't want to approach the water.'

One thing Maya did want to do, however, was play ball. A large part of the reason Gaz had chosen her was that she was ball obsessed. That drive to play is vitally important for a detection dog – or any sort of working dog, really – because the promise of play is their motivation to work, with a few minutes of playtime their reward for a job well done.

'You select them because they're absolutely ball or toy obsessed. You want the dog that, at a party, will bring you a ball, and if you stop throwing the ball they'll bring you a stick, and if you stop throwing the stick they'll bring you a leaf, and if you stop throwing the leaf they'll frantically go around the table to find something else that you can throw,' says Romane.

'You can't really ruin that obsession. You can take the dog home and have lots of cuddles and treat them as a pet, but as soon as they're back in work mode and you take out that toy that they really want, they are back into it.

'They need to be rewarded every day. They're playing dogs and they need to play all day, otherwise it's not fair. They're not interested in a salary at the end of the month.'

Romane had been told that Maya was a mix of working breeds. It was only years later that she discovered that was not the case at all.

'We were at an RSPCA occasion and some people came up to us that had a dog that was the spitting image of Maya. The same colouring, the same spots – she's got very spotty feet. They said, "You've got a lovely blue merle border collie,"' she says. 'A lot of people had told me she was a crossbreed and they said, "No, she's purebred, but it's a working line.'

Though she knew Maya was incredible, purebred or not, the comment was something of a revelation for Romane, because by then she was more than familiar with Maya's incredible work ethic. She'd even wondered if she might have been a farm dog in a former life, such was her drive to have a job to do. Knowing she was a border collie – a dog bred to herd livestock in the hilly border region between

England and Scotland – went some way to explaining why Maya was so uncannily good at what she did.

Because by that stage she was a fully trained koala-scat detection dog – and the success Romane had found thanks to Maya's sensitive nose was putting human capabilities to shame.

While Gaz had done some odour training with Maya, her training began in earnest in Romane's backyard. Familiarising her with the pungent smell of koala scat was easy, and she picked it up in no time. It was as if she had found her purpose in life. Romane would hide the pellets around her property and Maya quickly zeroed in on them.

Then, to establish just how much better Maya was at the task than a human, Romane put herself to the test. She asked a colleague, researcher Russell Miller, to hide scats in the bush, and set about finding them.

'I was playing hide-and-seek with poo, testing how many I found and how many I missed, so I could compare that with how many times Maya would miss a scat before she found it,' she says. 'In science it's very important to know how good and bad you are, and the limitations of your methods.'

Once Maya had the poo part down pat, Romane had to get her used to working in the great outdoors. With all its sounds, smells and potential hazards, that would be more challenging.

'That's the hardest part with rescue dogs, because they can have a lot of fear. I spent a lot of months training her outside so she would be happy in the bush,' Romane says. 'I had to take it quite slow, because I didn't know what her reaction would be.'

She drilled Maya on recall training, ensuring that she would always come when Romane called her, and then focused on teaching the clever collie an emergency stop. That was essential in the event Maya ever encountered an animal that wasn't a koala, such as a deadly snake.

'Detection dogs aren't interested in snakes, so they don't investigate, but if they haven't seen the snake they can step on it,' she says. 'I was really lucky that Maya never had the temperament of wanting to chase other animals. It was crucial. You cannot deploy a dog in the bush unless you're certain they're not going to hurt wildlife.'

While Maya's training was well in hand, Romane was also patiently waiting for state government approval to take the brainy border collie into the bush, to train with koala scat in actual koala habitat. Dogs are prohibited in national parks and other areas deemed to be of ecological importance.

Wading through the bureaucracy proved to be the most time-consuming aspect of the entire process, Romane says. 'You can imagine people's reactions when I was telling them, "I've got this dog and I want to take her into the bush to find koalas." It had never been done in Queensland before.'

At last the necessary permits were granted and Maya could swap the backyard for the wilderness. It was her first real test: would she find it just as easy to sniff out the precious poo amid the leaf litter and myriad other aromas of the forest?

'She was really good. Because she wasn't missing many scats, it convinced me that this was an accurate way of doing things,' says Romane. 'The next step was to see if she was better at it than humans, because that was the current method we were using.'

Maya had already outperformed Romane in that regard, but she needed a larger sample size to be sure the dog's performance wasn't just a fluke. To do that, she dispatched a team of researchers to multiple sites and had them search for koala scats with the naked eye. She then went with Maya to search the same sites.

When she compared the results, what she found was staggering: Maya's success rate showed that koalas were using the sites 30 per cent more than the humans had found. She was also twenty times faster than the human team.

'That was a really big surprise. I didn't expect such a difference in accuracy,' she says. 'If you can't even know that koalas are there 30 per cent of the time, you're going to really struggle to protect them.

'Relying on eyesight is really not efficient at all. As soon as a scat is covered by leaf litter, it's invisible to us. But for a dog, the scent cone – the pattern formed by an odour as it's carried away from the source – doesn't get obscured,' she says.

She also found that Maya performed better when off-leash. In fact, the only time she *didn't* locate the scats was when she was leashed with Romane as her handler.

'She's a very soft dog and, if the leash got tangled, it would tug at her neck. She would interpret that as a correction from me and she would obey me rather than take me to the scats,' she explains. 'I thought, *I'm going to drop the leash and see how she does*, and then she found the poo 100 per cent of the time.'

Romane got the sense that Maya was thankful to be out in the bush, working; glad to have been plucked from the pound and given a second chance at life.

'It feels like she's grateful. She's very motivated and always wants to do her best. She's a very happy dog who always looks at the bright side. You look at her in the morning and she's just happy for it to be today,' she says. 'I have a feeling that she was always an awesome dog and I just cannot believe that anyone would let go of her, but it's my luck that they did.'

The results of the experiment filled Romane with confidence in Maya's abilities, but she was still without a research position that would allow her to further develop Maya as a conservation dog. She didn't have any funding and was paying for the entire project out of her own pocket. She was spending hours applying for science grants, but had yet to be successful.

So she decided to start speaking publicly about what Maya could do. She gave lectures about detection dogs and non-invasive search techniques, hoping that academia, government agencies or private industry would take notice.

'I started doing a lot of public talks and telling people, "This is a really good method, and not only that but the method you're currently using is not good at all,"' says Romane. 'It started to make waves.'

Associate Professor Celine Frere, a friend who worked at the University of the Sunshine Coast (USC), suggested that Romane apply to join the faculty as an adjunct appointee, a researcher appointed to contribute their specialist expertise to a particular university department or research area.

So she did just that. In 2014, Romane arranged a demonstration of Maya's detection skills for a university panel that included the pro-vice-chancellor. When the big day arrived, the conditions couldn't have been worse.

'It was a very rainy, sad day. We wanted to take them into the bush but it was so rainy that we had to do the demonstration on a little patio, and there weren't any koala scats to be found,' she says.

Her colleague, Russell, had a container of koala scats as backup. He prepared to hide them in the vicinity while Maya and Romane waited about fifty metres away, facing the other way to ensure they didn't sneak a peek.

'All of the people we had invited to watch the demonstration were looking at me. Russell had just untwisted the lid of the little container when Maya turned around and looked at them,' she says. 'They all spotted that Maya had smelled it as soon as the container was opened. We came closer and Maya indicated on the scats. Everybody was very impressed.'

Nobody more so than the head honcho himself. 'The pro-vice-chancellor had, many years ago, started his own career looking for kangaroo poo. In all the fields he could have worked and all the careers he could have had, he started as an ecologist on roo poo,' she laughs. 'He said, "I would have loved to have had a dog like Maya during my PhD." He was already very, very aware of the problems ecologists have finding wildlife.'

He gave Romane and Maya the green light: they could join the university and continue trying to secure funding as a project supported by the institution.

'Every good story is a mix of hard work and luck, and we got a stroke of luck that day,' says Romane. 'You need someone that gets excited about your project.'

It wasn't quite full steam ahead from that very moment – it was another two years before Romane was finally able to secure grant funding – but she now had considerably more breathing room to develop and expand the project. More importantly, she had the belief and backing of a renowned research institution.

With her colleague Celine, in 2015 Romane co-founded the not-for-profit USC Detection Dogs for Conservation (DDC) team. Russell Miller became the team's dog trainer. Maya, of course, was the team's founding dog.

There would be no stopping the determined rescue dog now.

Today, Maya is a senior dog. If the original estimate of her age was correct she is now around ten years old, but it's possible she is even older.

'She's ten if we're lucky; if we're unlucky she's probably fourteen,' says Romane.

Just don't bother trying to explain to Maya that she's an elderly lady – she's simply not interested. She has arthritis and had surgery not long ago to repair torn tendons in her paw, but she is adamantly not ready for retirement.

'This breed of dog – and I feel this with Maya – stays really young in their heads. I don't think she feels her age. She still wants to play. Her mind wants to do the work, but her body probably needs to be slowing down,' Romane says.

'She still wants to go to work every day. She comes to the car and looks at me expectantly and is very upset with me if I don't take her. She will continue for as long as she wants it.'

When she isn't working, Maya is every bit the adored pet. She lives at home with Romane and spends her downtime doing all the normal dog stuff, including going to the beach, now that she has conquered her fear of the ocean.

Romane has faced criticism from other scientists who believe that blurring the lines between working dog and pet can confuse a dog and compromise their abilities in the field. After all, it is often destructive or compulsive behaviour at home that leads to pet dogs being surrendered and retrained as detection dogs in the first place.

But Romane simply couldn't come to terms with working so closely with Maya and then keeping her at arm's length when they were off the clock.

'People told me, "Romane, you are mad. You are going to destroy this dog – her drive will disappear." I thought,

Maybe so, but I'm not prepared to compromise on my ethics. Maya is actually very relaxed outside work. If I just want to hang out and have a rest, she'll just sit at my feet and have a snooze, but if I look like I'm going to touch the leash and take her for a walk, she will be very encouraging.

'She's a very lovely dog, which is rare in a detection dog. Sometimes they're "too much". But she's never too much – she never barks or chews. She's kind to other animals. She's probably a little bit too friendly with the cat – she considers the cat to be her best friend, but the cat isn't convinced.'

Maya is the matriarch of a team that now includes three other conservation dogs, two of which are also approaching senior status: Baxter, a six-year-old border collie cross; Billie-Jean, an Australian koolie who's also six; and Bear, the hero bushfire dog who went viral. All the dogs are rescues.

Bear is the only one of the quartet that is trained to find live koalas. That skill is a new string to the DDC team's bow, and it came about as a result of a partnership with the International Fund for Animal Welfare (IFAW).

'Maya has seen some koalas in trees, though we would like it if she never comes face to face with a koala. But there are occasions where the scats are not enough and you want to find a koala,' says Romane.

'In Australia we do a lot of controlled burning and the last thing you want to do is burn an area where there are koalas. Or sometimes a koala gets hurt on the road and they run away, and you need to find them. For research, sometimes you want to know how they move so you need to find the actual koala and attach a GPS.'

While the younger team members tackle these new branches of conservation detection, Maya, the doyenne of the group, continues to sniff out scats and provide researchers with valuable tools to help Australia's emblematic marsupial.

Most importantly, she continues to be a role model for how to be a boss at work and a perfect pet at home. 'She's the best dog of all the dogs in the whole wide universe. That's not me being biased at all – she just is.' Romane laughs.

For Romane, dogs in general – and Maya in particular – provide an ideal example of how to age gracefully.

'I don't think they care how old they are, and I don't think we should care either. Their personality is what matters, not their age. They are who they are,' she says. 'I never see Maya as an old dog. I see her as a friend, an amazing colleague, and a wonderfully happy personality.'

We should all take a (eucalyptus) leaf out of Maya's book.

Brook

The dog who saved the day

Sydney is renowned for its balmy, subtropical climate. The summer heat stretches well into autumn, with the mercury soaring again come early spring. The city's hundred-plus ocean and harbourside beaches teem with sunseekers all year round, while verdant suburban parks come alive with the sound of impromptu football games and the scent of barbecue smoke well into the long evenings.

Its global reputation as an oasis of endless summer means Sydney's winter chill can catch people off guard. Venture out without a jacket on a sunny July morning and you're likely to regret it by the afternoon. Even lifelong Sydneysiders can find themselves ill prepared for the intense cold that can descend midyear, shivering in the bitter winds that sweep down from the Blue Mountains and buffet the Pacific coastline.

This was the predicament Charlene Meade found herself in late one frigid August afternoon in 2015.

Charlene, then eighty-four, had taken her Shetland sheepdogs, Brook and Piper, to the Centennial Parklands just east of central Sydney. It was their daily ritual: they visited the park every afternoon for some fresh air and exercise, and so that long-time obedience competitor Charlene could run the dogs through their training drills.

The preceding days had been wet, and the forecast promised more rain a little later that day. Indeed, the clouds gathering over the 189-hectare park looked ominously leaden already. But Charlene wasn't overly concerned. It was too cold to stay out long anyway, and she was sure they'd be snug and warm at home in nearby Vaucluse before the rain started.

She unclipped the dogs' leashes so they could sniff to their little hearts' content, following her electric wheel-chair. Brook and Piper were obedience champions with excellent recall; if they wandered too far afield, a word from her would bring them trotting back to her side.

Charlene, a silver-medal-winning Paralympian, was at that time one of the world's oldest living paraplegics from trauma. In 1946, at the age of fourteen, she was thrown from a horse while racing a school friend. The fall caused a fracture in Charlene's spine at the T5 vertebra, paralysing her from the chest down.

After decades using a series of cumbersome manual chairs, her electric wheelchair was Charlene's ticket to freedom. According to her daughter, Angela Meade, 'She used it like a four-wheel drive.'

'She'd go shooting along the footpaths and through the parks. It used to tip over every now and then,' Angela says, laughing. 'Her handbag would go flying, but she had trained one of the dogs to go and bring over her phone so she could call for help.'

So that day, Charlene didn't think twice about steering the wheelchair off the park's marked paths and onto the grass in leisurely pursuit of the dogs. She was confident the machine, like her clever pets, was up to any task she could throw at it.

Any task, she soon discovered, except conquering wet leaves.

As Charlene traversed a grassy corner of the park, her wheelchair hit a patch of soggy foliage under a towering oak tree. And stopped.

She tried to accelerate forward, but the wheels simply spun in place. And spun . . . and spun. Each revolution gouged a deeper groove into the sodden earth.

At first, Charlene was merely annoyed as her wheelchair sank further into the mud. She had been in similar predicaments plenty of times, but she was frustrated that her pleasant park sojourn would now be longer and more challenging than anticipated.

Twenty minutes later, however, the chair was still stuck fast. She yelled for help but got no response. She could see people in the distance, but there was nobody within earshot. It was growing even colder, the shadows lengthening and the clouds darkening.

A tiny tendril of fear unfurled in her gut. Charlene shivered.

How was she going to get herself out of this one?

Charlene Meade was not always a dog lover. In fact, as a very young child, she was terrified of canines. But her mother, Phyllis, felt the best way for her daughter to overcome this fear was to confront it head on.

'Mum decided the best way to get over being frightened was to get a puppy. At six or seven I got a puppy called Jimmy,' Charlene, who was born Charlene Todman, told the Pets4Life website in 2016.

She adored Jimmy so much that she decided she wanted to become a veterinarian when she finished school. Charlene also decided that she would never be without a dog, and that her ideal breed was a collie.

But her accident in 1946 changed those plans. There were few, if any, spinal cord injury rehabilitation facilities in those days. The hospital where she initially received treatment was run by nuns and did not have a spinal care centre. Charlene's school was not wheelchair accessible, forcing her to complete her secondary education via correspondence.

Charlene decided to focus all of her energy on becoming as independent as possible as a paraplegic and wheelchair user. She replaced her unwieldy wooden wheelchair with a more modern, collapsible model, and took typing courses, which helped her to find a job.

She also became an accomplished athlete and in 1951 was the first Australian woman to compete at the Stoke Mandeville Games in England, which later became the International Wheelchair and Amputee World Games and were the forerunner to the Paralympic Games. Charlene finished second in women's archery, and returned in 1959 to compete in swimming, archery and javelin. She won a silver medal in table tennis at the 1974 games.

But for the first twelve years after her injury Charlene was without a dog, and she desperately missed having a four-legged friend. 'There was no rehabilitation in those days. I initially had to sit in a big wooden and cane wheelchair, which was very awkward to manoeuvre,' she told Pets4Life. 'I realised then that, with that wheelchair, a collie dog would be too big for me.'

That changed in 1955, when she married Eric Meade. The couple had two children, Angela and Stuart, and after becoming a mum, Charlene decided the time was right to have a dog again.

The family visited their local RSPCA shelter and adopted Benjy, a corgi cross who became a much-loved family member. When Benjy passed away, Charlene's thoughts drifted back to the dog breed she had always loved: collies. She knew a Lassie-type rough collie would be too big for her to manage, but that was okay. She had discovered the next best thing.

'I used to love the Royal Easter Show in Sydney, and I still do. When I was sixteen, I was taken to the Easter Show. That's when I saw the Shetland sheepdogs. It was love at first sight. I thought, *I'm going to get one of those,*' she told Pets4Life.

Commonly known as the Sheltie, the Shetland sheepdog is a herding breed that originated in Scotland's Shetland Islands in the early twentieth century. Despite looking like a miniature Lassie, the Sheltie is not a direct descendant of the rough collie but a mix of diminutive Scottish collies and King Charles spaniels.

Weighing between 5 and 11 kilograms, Shelties are a much more compact version of their rough collie look-alikes, which can weigh more than 30 kilograms. As well as being hardworking, friendly and athletic, the breed is known for their quick brains, ranking sixth out of the 138 breeds tested for animal intelligence by expert Dr Stanley Coren. He found that an average Sheltie could understand a new command in fewer than five repetitions and would obey a command the first time it was given 95 per cent of the time.

In other words, they're exactly the type of dog that suits a wheelchair user with young children.

'By the time I was around 30, I decided to get a Sheltie for the family. My husband and our children didn't mind [so] I got a puppy, Zoe, with white collar markings, from a breeder,' Charlene said. 'She needed a lot brushing.'

Angela agrees that the Sheltie was the perfect breed for her fiercely independent mum. 'They're small, clever, eager to learn and easy to handle. Anything bigger she would have struggled to control.'

That eagerness to learn was enormously important to

Charlene, then still using a manual wheelchair, because she needed her pets to be adaptable and well trained. When their first dog, Benjy, had joined the family, Charlene had pivoted in her athletic pursuits and ventured into the world of dog sports, starting with obedience trialling. She intended to compete with her Sheltie, too.

'Mum always had to have pets around her. She would accidentally run over their paws with the wheelchair, the same as she did to us children. The dogs had to learn,' says Angela. 'The obedience training allowed them to live quite happily in the house. She trained them to do things for her as well, like collecting the newspaper.'

Charlene's foray into obedience trialling had been quite accidental. A friend suggested to her that she meet another friend's daughter, who was also a wheelchair user. That young lady had a Pekingese dog that she took to training. Charlene decided to go along to her club in Lindfield, on Sydney's North Shore, for a look.

'Before I knew it, I was signed up,' she told Pets4Life. 'In those days, the only dog trials for crossbreeds were the RSPCA trials. They had a trial only every three months. Benjy did well for a few years in dog trialling.'

When Zoe came along, Charlene swapped the RSPCA events for purebred obedience trials.

Angela says her mum was so passionate about the sport that she was soon attending training several days a week.

'She went through various different clubs. She would chop and change depending on what the dog was learning.

She used to drive for miles.' She laughs. 'It depended what level of training she was at and what she was doing.'

Charlene also put in hours of work at home and during the daily park outings that became a lifelong routine. She saw any brief pocket of time as an opportunity for her dogs to learn.

'If there were jumps to learn, she'd set them up in the front garden. She'd always take her dogs up to the park in the afternoon to have a run around with the other dogs,' says Angela. 'If she got there early she'd take them around the corner and train them to do something.'

Though she loved it, the competitive world of dog sports was not always easy for Charlene. In obedience competitions, handlers may only speak to their dogs to issue set commands, which the dog must then perform. They are not allowed to communicate via any other method at any time. But Charlene's dogs were so well trained and performed so well in trials that some club officials were convinced she was cheating by using hand signals.

The suggestion was both insulting and preposterous, says Angela. 'The judges always thought she was somehow giving the dogs hand signals while pushing her wheelchair. They thought Mum wouldn't be able to control a dog *and* push a wheelchair. It took a long time for the trialling community to understand that she was so busy pushing herself that there was no way she could be giving the dogs hand signals.'

Unfortunately for those judges, they were clearly not aware of everything Charlene had overcome in her life.

Or the fact that when she set her mind to something she had a laser focus that ensured she achieved it. Their accusations only drove Charlene to become even better at what she did.

'She got over that, but it was quite difficult for her in the beginning. Like anything Mum did, she just got on with it. She would prove that both she and the dog could do it,' says Angela. 'She would do anything to prove a point. She was very strong minded.'

And she would soon welcome a dog whose tenacity more than matched her own.

Zoe wasn't an only dog for very long. She was soon joined by Candy, also a Sheltie – Charlene had by now pledged her lifelong allegiance to the breed. Meggsie the cat, known to all as Puss, completed the menagerie.

Charlene loved her household ark, and always preferred to have two dogs at a time, especially after Eric passed away in 1996.

'I like having two dogs because they keep each other company when I go out,' she told Pets4Life in 2016. 'Puss was standoffish with me, but after a year or two I started cuddling him before I fed him. Now he waits for his cuddle before he gets his dinner. Puss will tell the dogs where to get off, [but] the dogs love the cat.'

Angela suspects the addition of Meggsie to the family was largely for her benefit. 'I was a cat person, so there was always a cat in the mix as well,' she says. 'The dogs were good to play with and they were all really well behaved. Zoe and Candy were really, really clever.'

And then came Brook, who Angela says was the smartest dog her mother ever owned. Brook arrived in 2004, at the age of two, after a short-lived career as a show dog. Zoe had passed away by then and Candy was getting old, so the young newcomer was to be her companion as well as Charlene's next training protégé.

Angela vividly recalls the day she met Brook. 'I remember this very skinny little terrified dog. She'd had a litter before she came.'

Whatever she'd endured in her former life, timid Brook already had the obedience basics down pat, and she had an unquenchable thirst for learning that Charlene had never encountered before.

'Mum wanted an older Sheltie so that she would already be fully house-trained and have a level of leash control so Mum could walk her,' says Angela. 'Brook was very clever. She was easy to train and she'd pick things up very quickly.'

Training with Charlene helped to cement Brook's attachment to her new mistress just as swiftly. 'Mum loved her dogs and had a close bond with all of them, but Brook just loved it. She could think outside the square and seemed to just know, *This thing needs to be done.*'

Brook was so proactive that she was something of a hindrance to her canine sibling Piper's progress when he joined the clan in 2011. Piper came from New Zealand where, like Brook, he'd had a brief and underwhelming career as a show dog. In Piper's case, a tooth that stuck out had cut short his time in the show ring. Charlene loved this so-called flaw, as well as Piper's 'lovely and affectionate' temperament.

For her part, Brook adored her new little brother too. 'Brook and Piper were more like mother and son. She decided he was her puppy,' says Angela. 'She would clean Piper's mouth and ears and treat him like her own baby.'

Piper was every bit as intelligent as Brook, but didn't have the same focus and attention span – which was fine by Brook, who was happy to complete Piper's training tasks for him. 'Mum would be trying to teach Piper something using an object and Piper would just stand there and look at her, so Brook would get fed up and pick it up and take it outside,' Angela says. 'Piper is also very trainable, but he gets bored very quickly.'

In an effort to retain Piper's attention, Charlene switched from traditional obedience to RallyO, a less formal version of the sport in which handlers are allowed to talk to their dogs in the ring, rather than only issuing the permitted commands. Piper enjoyed this new sport a little better, but eventually Charlene concluded that he simply didn't like competition obedience.

'Mum stopped taking him to obedience training because he'd get into the ring and get too excited and distracted and disappear,' says Angela.

Charlene certainly didn't mind that Piper wouldn't be an obedience champion like Brook. For her, obedience trialling was about keeping her pets healthy, happy and mentally stimulated. She felt it was especially important for Brook, who was by then well into her senior years.

Charlene never stopped learning either, believing that maintaining an active mind was a fundamental part of ageing well. Angela was constantly amazed at how full Charlene's calendar was. She was forever signing up for new activities, and remained a tireless volunteer in the disability sector. In 2008, Charlene was awarded a Medal of the Order of Australia for her efforts in serving Australia's disability community.

'She had the dogs and they kept her company. She was always busy and was never lonely,' she says. 'How she did everything I have no idea, because I'm up to my eyeballs living with just a dog and a cat!'

Besides, there were always new things to teach Brook. By 2015 her star pupil was officially an elderly lady, having turned twelve, but she was showing no signs of growing tired of training and acquiring new skills. She was indispensable to Charlene around the house. 'Mum and Dad became hard of hearing later in life, so the dogs learned to bark when the phone was ringing,' Angela says.

Obedience accolades and alerting her owner to a ringing telephone were impressive, but it's what Brook did next that would make headlines and earn her the title of hero dog.

Charlene was a positive thinker through and through, but her situation in Centennial Parklands would test anybody's optimism. Her heavy electric wheelchair was completely bogged in the soft earth and slippery leaf litter. Time was marching on and the winter air was growing colder with every passing minute.

Making matters worse, having gone 'off road', she was in a section of the park with little foot traffic. The chances of being happened upon by a passerby were slim.

'From long experience, I am generally very cautious in such terrain, but on this day, I misjudged the lie of the land,' she told Pets4Life.

Charlene could see a group of people enjoying a picnic at a table in the distance and yelled for help. Brook and Piper, sensing their owner's distress, began to bark furiously – as Charlene herself had trained them to do in an emergency.

But either the languid lunchers weren't paying attention, or they were just too far away to hear a shouting senior citizen and her two perturbed pets.

Charlene was in quite the pickle. She had to admit she was worried.

But it wasn't the first time she had found herself stranded, says Angela. 'Mum was very good at getting stuck. We'd all had to pull her out of the garden at some point because her front wheels would get stuck. She wouldn't pay attention to the ground conditions and she'd get bogged.'

This time, however, the intrepid adventurer couldn't rely on one of her children to extract her from trouble. The only tools at her disposal were her dogs, and they couldn't do anything besides bark.

Or could they?

Suddenly, as if responding to an unspoken instruction from Charlene, Brook took off. She raced towards the picnickers and parked herself next to them on the damp grass, still barking as though her life depended on it – or the life of the person she loved most in the world.

The people looked at Brook, bemused, but nobody got up. Even after she had yapped at them for fifteen minutes, no one seemed to wonder why a little dog might be on her own in the park, on a bleak winter afternoon, barking frantically.

So Brook kept barking, and barking, and barking. Nothing.

Then Brook changed tack. She deliberately stopped barking and charged towards the group instead. Finally, that got her some attention. One man looked up long enough to see Charlene in the distance, waving madly. He waved cheerily back and then turned his attention back to his companions.

As she had often demonstrated while waiting for Piper to master a new trick, Brook wasn't always the most patient of pooches. It's easy to imagine that she might at that moment have been thinking something along the lines of, *You're just not getting it!*

Watching from her boggy position, Charlene shared her dog's frustration. 'I thought, *Oh dear, that's not the idea at all,*' she later recalled.

Now Brook got to her feet, barking at the group once again, and began to back slowly away, heading in Charlene's direction. Finally, mercifully, the penny seemed to drop for the man who'd waved at Charlene.

He stood up and followed Brook. He reached a relieved Charlene, who explained her problem, and he was able to help free her wheelchair from the quagmire and get her back onto solid ground within minutes.

Sticking diligently to the paved paths, Charlene, Brook and Piper made it back to the car just as the heavens opened, drenching the park in an icy downpour. 'Just as well, because electric wheelchairs definitely don't like getting wet,' she reported. 'Brook got an extra hug that night for rescuing her mum from a soggy night – or worse – in the park.'

The man who had finally come to Charlene's aid was also full of praise for Brook. 'He rightly pointed out that, "If it hadn't been for your clever dog, you might have been stuck here for a very long time,"' Charlene told Sydney's *Daily Telegraph*.

But she didn't need a stranger to tell her what she already knew: her clever old dog had saved the day, and quite possibly Charlene's life. Who knows what might have become of her had she been stuck out there in those wild conditions as night fell. Brook had made sure Charlene didn't have to find out.

Even more impressive was the fact that Brook had acted on her own initiative. Charlene may have trained her to bark for attention in an emergency, but she had not taught her to physically go and seek help. That ingenuity was all Brook's own.

'Brook hadn't done anything like that before. She just took it upon herself to do it. She was very clever like that,' says Angela. 'I think Mum was impressed because it was just so out of the ordinary. There was no way she could have directed the dog to do it. Brook knew there was something wrong, but to this day I don't know how she thought, *Let's go and do this.*'

Charlene felt that Brook deserved wider recognition for her amazing rescue effort, so she wrote up the tremendous tale and sent it off to the Royal Agricultural Society of NSW's Canine Hero Awards.

In April 2016, Brook took out the Companion Dog Award category, which is presented to a dog in private owner-ship that 'through a single act or over a period of time has displayed in an exceptional way the human–animal bond'.

Fittingly, Charlene and Brook received the award from then Governor-General Sir Peter Cosgrove at the Sydney Royal Easter Show – the very place where Charlene had fallen in love with collie dogs some fifty years earlier.

Angela says her mum was tickled pink by the accolade. 'Mum always felt that old dogs can do so much,' she says. 'She found that keeping their brain going is so impor-tant. She never just sat around, so the dogs couldn't sit around – they had to go out with her and run around.'

It was undoubtedly that unflagging enthusiasm for life that enabled Brook to save Charlene from danger that day.

Charlene, Piper and Brook continued to be an indefati-gable trio for another two years after Brook's heroism in Centennial Parklands. They kept training and visiting the park most afternoons, with Brook's repertoire of tricks and skills always expanding, though she retired from competition.

Then, in September 2018, Charlene fell ill with cellulitis, a bacterial skin infection. Two weeks later she passed away from complications arising from the condition. She was eighty-seven.

After her mum died, Angela moved into Charlene's Vaucluse home to look after Brook, Piper and Meggsie. 'I had three little shadows following me around. I kept the same routine, taking them to the park every afternoon.'

Thankfully, her mum had left detailed instructions for their care. 'Because Mum used to go into hospital pretty often, there was always a list for whoever came in to look after the pets on what to feed them, so that made it easier to take over,' says Angela. 'It certainly wasn't just dog food – they'd eat raw kangaroo and cooked vegetables. They were exceptionally healthy dogs.'

Nevertheless, Charlene's passing was understandably difficult for everyone, including her pets. Angela later relocated with the animals to Port Macquarie on the NSW mid-north coast, feeling that a fresh start would be good for all of them. 'Mum had sometimes been in hospital for up to three months, so they were used to her being away – but she always came back. Moving helped them to understand that she wasn't coming back.'

Brook was about fifteen years old when Charlene passed away. She had arthritis and a handful of other health niggles, but she had exceeded the average Sheltie lifespan of twelve to fourteen years. Brook died peacefully on Boxing Day 2018.

Piper, now eight, and fifteen-year-old Meggsie are still going strong and enjoying their sea change, and Angela has been glad of their company as she settles into her new home. 'They've had a lot of change in a short space of time, and they still follow me around. Piper thinks he's the boss, but the cat continues to boss everyone around.'

There's a delightful symmetry in Angela's new life with her mum's old dog. With Piper by her side, she goes out and embraces life – just as Charlene always did with Brook, and the dogs that came before her.

The story of Charlene Meade and her remarkable dogs is proof of that old saying, 'There's life in the old dog yet.'

Old dogs have so much to teach us all about life, if only we're willing to learn.

Chloe Bear

The dog who found her way home

When it comes to dogs, there are two universal truths.

The first is that you will never forget your first dog. It's impossible. It's a profound bond, the first time you receive that unconditional love, absolute trust, and unshakeable loyalty. It changes a person like no other relationship.

Whether she came to you as a child or an adult, shared your life for fifteen years or fifteen minutes, the first four-legged friend to leave paw prints on your heart will remain there forever. That's just a fact.

The second universal truth is this: the dog chooses you. Sure, it *seems* like we make the decision, because we like to imagine that we're in charge. We spend hours, days, weeks, poring over the websites of dog rescue groups and shelters. We diligently fill out adoption application forms. Or we thoroughly research our breed of choice, ask responsible breeders the necessary questions about lineage and health, linger on waiting lists. We tell ourselves that we are in control.

Her arrival might have been months in the making, but make no mistake, when that cautious rescue dog or wriggling puppy is in your arms at last, it's because she chose you. The dog makes the call. Always.

And once a dog has made that choice, there isn't much that can un-make it. Not time, distance or separation. When she has picked her human, she will do everything possible to stay by her human's side. Dogs, after all, are supremely powerful, and a little bit magical.

This is especially true of Chloe Bear, a little dog ostensibly chosen *for* her young human who was, in fact, clearly the one that made the choice.

Chloe's owner, Nicole Grimes, comes from a family of dog lovers. She and her husband, Isaiah, and their young kids, Violet, Jonah and Noah, dote on their spunky one-year-old Shih tzu, Itsy. And Nicole's parents, Michelle and Mark Bush, have a loveable Labrador named Kaia; the latest in a long line of adored family pets.

But Chloe was that all-important first dog – the first that was truly Nicole's.

She arrived in the northern autumn of 2006, when Nicole was a nine-year-old only child growing up in Marianna, Pennsylvania. While many only children wish for a sibling – and Nicole would get one when her brother, Jake, was born the following January – what she longed for was a four-legged playmate.

'I would talk to my nana on the phone all the time and

tell her, "I wish I had a little fluffy dog to come home from school to every day." Like a little friend,' Nicole says. 'I guess I was a bit lonely.'

Unbeknownst to Nicole, her grandmother, Jane, took her pleas to heart – and then decided to take matters into her own hands.

'One day my mum picked me up from school, which was kind of unusual, because she didn't pick me up that often. Nana was in the car, and on her lap was this little fluffy black puppy with a pink bow in her hair,' she recalls. 'I was just in shock. I was so excited! I didn't know I was getting a dog. I would talk about wanting one, but I didn't know it was going to be a thing.'

The puppy, who Nicole quickly decided to call Chloe Bear, was a pomapoo, a cross between the Pomeranian and toy poodle breeds. She was fluffy almost to the point of (adorable) scruffiness, like the titular star of Lynley Dodd's Hairy Maclary children's books.

And just like Hairy Maclary, Chloe had a mischievous streak. 'She liked socks – if you played with a sock with her she would love that,' Nicole recalls. 'We have home videos of me and my brother when he was a toddler, playing with her with a sock. He loved her too.'

But Chloe quickly became Nicole's best buddy. 'My parents enjoyed her too, but she and I were the ones that really clicked. We were best friends. I loved her. We'd be lying on the couch, watching TV, and she would lie on my stomach. If I started to fall asleep she'd start licking my face to alert me.'

Chloe was just about perfect, but she did have one naughty habit: she liked to bark. No matter how hard they tried, the family just couldn't convince Chloe to be a little less vocal.

'She was a yippy little thing.' Nicole laughs.

The author W Bruce Cameron once said, 'When you adopt a dog, you have a lot of very good days and one very bad day.' The day Chloe came into her life was the happiest young Nicole could remember. Sadly, it was Chloe's barking, combined with a change in employment for Nicole's father, that would lead to the most devastating day she had yet experienced.

In 2011, when Nicole was fourteen, her dad got a job in customer service that meant he would be working from home; Chloe's noisy behaviour put that job in jeopardy. 'He wasn't allowed a dog that barked, and he didn't want to lose the job, because it was a good opportunity.'

Four years after Chloe Bear had joined the family, Nicole's parents made the heartbreaking decision to rehome her.

Nicole doesn't remember much about how they broke the sad news to her. 'I think my dad just said something along the lines of, "I don't want to lose this opportunity" and that Chloe would need to go to a home that was more suitable for her,' she says.

But Nicole does remember how the announcement made her feel. It hit her like a punch in the gut. She felt powerless and heartsick at the thought of losing her fluffy best friend, although she knew how important her father's

Kim and John Murphy knew that Haole loved adventure, but they could never have imagined that even as a senior dog his passion for surfing would help so many children experience the magic of surf therapy. *(Erik Eiser)*

Maggie was unofficially the world's oldest dog – and officially dairy farmer Brian McLaren's best mate for nearly thirty years. *(Brian McLaren)*

Chilli was already a senior when he found fame in the popular TV drama *A Place to Call Home*. But his owner, dog trainer Vicki Austin, knew he was a star the moment she saw him. *(Vicki Austin)*

Chaser, the amazing 'talking' border collie, could identify over a thousand different objects. Though their incredible work didn't come to worldwide attention until both were seniors, she and her owner, canine-cognition expert John Pilley, shared a lifelong love affair.

(Pilley Bianchi)

It was a dark and stormy night when emaciated senior street dog Suzy sought refuge in the home of Jack and Emily Jokinen. What happened next changed not only their lives but inspired hundreds to rescue dogs of their own. *(Jack Jokinen)*

Trained to sniff out koala habitats, rescue dog Maya is working as tirelessly as ever in her senior years. *(Marie Colibri)*

Plucky little sheltie Brook was trained to assist her owner, Charlene Meade. But when Charlene was caught up in an emergency, Brook's ingenuity in getting her out of trouble amazed everyone.

(Angela Meade)

As a child, Nicole Grimes's heart broke when she had to rehome her beloved dog, Chloe Bear. She assumed she would never see her again – but almost a decade later, fate had other ideas. *(Nicole Grimes)*

In nearly twenty years of outback adventures with Larry Mitchell, Holly never put a paw wrong – until one day the elderly pooch simply vanished without a trace.

(Larry Mitchell; Kelsey Reid/ Kalgoorlie Miner)

His long life was marked by calamity and disaster, including losing both eyes, but Arnie the poodle never lost his joyful spirit. Even today he still inspires his owner, artist Jane Canfield.

(Jane Canfield)

He was a big old boy whose puppy-like spirit led him into trouble more than once, but on one occasion it took a whole team of people – and other dogs – to rescue Puppy the Pyrenean Mountain Dog. *(Jim Branson, Three Retrievers Lost Pet Rescue)*

A shock diagnosis meant Magnus the senior greyhound wouldn't have as long with his adoptive owners, Kristan and Jason Norris, as they'd hoped. So they created a bucket list designed to fill his days with fun, including a ride in a police car and eating fish and chips on the beach. *(Archer Imagery)*

For seventeen years, Jonesy the Australian Lions Hearing Dog has given his Deaf owner, Megan Grant, peace of mind at home, the opportunity to travel, and boundless love.

(Megan Grant)

It seemed like Rachel Devenish-Meares's adored white German shepherd, Kato, would not achieve much in the world of competitive dog sports. But remarkably – at the age when most competition dogs are thinking about retiring – he hit his stride, going on to win a string of titles. *(Tina Dial, Pawsnap Pet Photography)*

Tamana is a senior amputee who was plucked from a life of hardship on the streets of Iran and transported to a loving temporary home in the US. Even on only two paws, she loves exploring nature with her foster family, but Tamana is still searching for her forever home.

(Elizabeth Waynick)

job was. Marianna's unemployment rate is higher than the national average; Nicole understood that her dad needed this job.

'I remember I felt sick to my stomach about it. I was so sad. I tried to talk him out of it, but I was just a kid so I couldn't do much, and I knew that he was trying to do what was best for our family,' she says.

In an effort to ease their daughter's anguish, Nicole's parents first rehomed Chloe with a neighbour. They thought that if she could still see her little dog every now and then, the loss wouldn't feel quite so raw.

But having Chloe close by only made it harder for Nicole. She was so near, and yet so far.

In the spring of 2011, the family persuaded the neighbour to return Chloe and decided instead to rehome her through their local no-kill shelter, the Washington Area Humane Society (WAHS).

In a sad irony, the friendship that had begun with Nicole and Chloe in the family car would end in the same place. While Nicole didn't want to participate in Chloe's surrender, she also didn't want her best friend to travel to the shelter without her, so she went along for the trip. It was, she says, the gloomiest car ride of her young life.

'This sounds so cliché, but it was a rainy day. It was starting to get dark out. I just remember this feeling of total misery,' says Nicole. 'I remember sitting in the back seat, feeling this pit of anxiety and sadness in my stomach. I didn't want to go in, so I stayed in the car. I didn't want to be a part of it, but I didn't have a choice.'

In the days and weeks that followed Chloe's departure, Nicole thought about her often. Virtually everything reminded her of her absent companion, from Chloe's birthday – 26 October – to a pair of socks.

'I would think about her randomly. I really did miss her and I was really sad about it,' she says.

A couple of months after Chloe was given up, Nicole's longing got the better of her and she called the WAHS. The news was both wonderful and awful.

'I called to see if she had been adopted, or to get some information about how she was doing. They said she had been adopted, but they couldn't give me any personal details about her new family.'

Marianna is a tiny town – in 2018, its population was less than 500 – but WAHS is the local shelter for every town in Washington County, which has more than 200,000 inhabitants. If Nicole harboured any hope of catching a glimpse of Chloe with her new family someday, they were quickly dashed. 'I wasn't really expecting her to turn up close to me. I didn't think I was going to be that lucky,' she says. 'Honestly, I didn't think I would ever see Chloe again.'

Nicole felt she had no choice but to accept the sad truth: she had loved Chloe with every fibre of her being, but her little dog was gone. All she could do was hope that Chloe had found a new home with people who deserved her and who would love her as much as Nicole had.

Scratch that – as much as Nicole *did*. Because she knew she wouldn't stop loving Chloe. Not ever.

*

A lot can happen in seven years. It certainly did for Nicole. By 2018, she was twenty-one, married to Isaiah, and mum to baby Violet. She was working as a pharmacy assistant, and the young family had moved thirty minutes east of Marianna to West Brownsville, an equally small town on the banks of the Monongahela River. She had also said a sad goodbye to her beloved grandmother; Jane passed away in early 2015.

Nicole's life was busy and full, but the hole that Chloe had left still remained. She still thought of her often, wondering what had become of her. Chloe would be an old dog by now – Nicole still wished her a silent 'happy birthday' on 26 October every year – and she hoped that, if she was still living, she was warm and loved and well looked after.

The Grimes family didn't have a dog at that stage, but Nicole and Isaiah thought they might start looking for a furry friend in six months or so, after Violet turned one and would be excited to grow up with a canine companion.

As is so often the case, however, the universe had other plans.

That January, in the middle of a bitterly cold Pennsylvania winter, a friend of Nicole's, Lacey, posted on Facebook that she was looking for a new home for her dog. The two women had recently connected on social media after meeting in a mothers' group, so it was the first time Nicole had heard about or seen pictures of Lacey's pets.

But immediately, there was something about the dog that seemed familiar.

'I saw that Lacey was trying to rehome this elderly dog because it wasn't getting along with her other dog. She was this little fluffy, old, grey dog and she didn't have any teeth,' Nicole recalls. 'I thought the dog was really cute and kind of familiar looking. It was just funny to me, like, *I had a dog that kind of looked like that.*'

Even more amazing was the fact that this senior lady was called Chloe, though Nicole didn't for a moment imagine the dog was Chloe Bear. 'It had been at least seven or eight years since I'd last seen my Chloe, so I didn't read too much into it. Chloe isn't the most unusual name for a dog. I just thought it was a coincidence,' she says.

But it was too big a coincidence for Nicole to ignore. She felt like fate was telling her to forget about waiting and open her heart to this dog that reminded her so much of *her* Chloe.

So, without really thinking about it, Nicole messaged Lacey. 'I'll take her.'

She didn't think twice, either, about whether the toothless senior pooch might arrive with other health problems. Whatever the little dog's issues, Nicole felt willing and able to handle them.

It's a view not shared by some people, if the number of senior dogs dumped and surrendered every year is any indication. That's an attitude Nicole doesn't understand. 'A lot of people only want to get a puppy – and it is nice to raise a puppy, I'm not going to deny that – but so many people don't even think about getting an older dog,' she says. 'It's lovely to adopt an older dog, because you're really helping out for the last years of their life. Plus, they're so sweet, and half the time they're already trained, so you don't have to worry about it.'

When she met Chloe, Nicole was even more confident that her spontaneous decision had been the right one. 'Lacey brought Chloe over to my house the next day. She was so friendly and such a loving dog right away. She was really sweet and her tail never stopped wagging.'

As their first day together continued, however, Nicole started to feel a little unsure. Not about keeping the dog – there was no doubt she was a sweetheart – but about Chloe's true identity.

The little dog wouldn't take her eyes off Nicole for a moment, and she had certain personality quirks that were uncannily similar to the dog she had farewelled years before.

'She was really clinging to me, and just different mannerisms she had and the way she acted made me suspicious,' Nicole says. 'I don't know if other dogs do this a lot, but my Chloe Bear used to walk around in a zillion circles before she'd go to the bathroom. Not once or twice – she'd walk around forever! This Chloe was doing that, too. When I saw it, my eyes got big and I was like, *This is odd.*'

But this Chloe couldn't possibly be Nicole's childhood dog, could she? The chances were surely one in several million. People simply didn't get a second chance with the dog they'd surrendered.

There was also the fact that, while senior Chloe certainly bore a striking resemblance to the dog Nicole remembered, there were marked differences. Young Chloe Bear had been almost entirely black; this Chloe was completely grey, and seemed much smaller than the dog Nicole had last seen at WAHS.

Still, she couldn't shake the feeling that maybe, somehow, the four-legged friend she had loved so fiercely, and whose loss she still mourned, was now in her living room.

'I really did start to think, *Maybe this is her*. My husband and my mum thought I was crazy. But when my parents and my brother came over, and Dad and I took Chloe outside, he saw what I saw and he was like, "Wait a minute . . ."'

That night, when the house was quiet and it was just Nicole and Chloe cuddling on the couch, she was left with no doubt.

'I was sitting there holding her and it was like she was hugging me. I felt it at that point,' she says. 'I knew.'

But she couldn't feel truly satisfied until she had proof that Chloe Bear really had come back. So the next day, Nicole's mum, Michelle, called WAHS.

'My Chloe was chipped, so Mum called the WAHS and got the chip number, then I took the "new" Chloe to the vet and they scanned her,' she says.

The vet technician began to read out the nine-digit microchip number.

Zero-two-four . . .

Nicole felt her heart skip a beat.

Zero-nine-nine . . .

Her breath caught in her throat.

Eight-one-one.

It was an exact match.

Tiny, grey, toothless Chloe and rambunctious, yippy, sock-loving Chloe Bear were one and the same.

The dog Nicole thought she would never see again had found her way home.

Though gut instinct had told her from the start that her new canine companion was her Chloe Bear, the confirmation left Nicole reeling. 'I was in a state of shock. In my heart I knew it was her, but it was mind blowing. I couldn't stop smiling. I felt like I was on cloud nine.' She laughs. 'It's probably the craziest thing that has ever happened to me.'

She couldn't help but feel that her late grandmother, Jane, had perhaps had a spiritual hand in bringing Chloe home. 'When she came back, it felt like a sign from my nana. It was really emotional for my mum.'

Verifying her microchip number also meant Nicole was able to find out what Chloe Bear's life had been like in the seven years they had been apart. Happily, the news was good.

After Nicole's family surrendered her, an elderly couple had adopted Chloe from WAHS. They doted on Chloe until they both passed away within a short period of time, at which point their daughter, who wasn't able to care for Chloe herself, set about finding a new home for her. Lacey was a friend of the couple's daughter, and so she took Chloe in.

Lacey had her for about a year. She would have loved to keep her permanently, but her other dog was not willing to accept a new housemate. Eventually, she had to concede that Chloe would be happier elsewhere. She appealed to her Facebook friends, hoping to find a suitable new home. One of those friends was, of course, Nicole.

Learning that the intervening years had been kind to Chloe was a comfort for Nicole. 'She went from me to the couple to my friend and then back to me, so she was not bounced to a million different homes,' she says. 'Lacey and I hadn't been Facebook friends for that long. She couldn't believe it either. I do wonder whether, if I'd been friends with her when she first adopted Chloe, I would have seen pictures and got suspicious earlier.'

And Nicole is sure that having only two homes after hers is what allowed Chloe Bear to remember her just as vividly as she recalled her fluffy playmate. Well, that and the fact that Chloe chose Nicole to be her human when both were just little girls.

'I fully believe in my heart that she did remember me, which is nice because I was just a kid at the time she was rehomed,' says Nicole. 'It's really unbelievable after all those years apart, but I truly believe that she knew it was me.'

It wasn't long before the local media got wind of Nicole and Chloe's serendipitous reunion. Then the national media picked up the story and before long the tale of the young woman who unknowingly adopted her childhood dog had gone globally viral. 'It was in newspapers, different magazines, different animal pages on social media. I got messages from several different countries. I couldn't even reply to all of them because there were just too many.'

While the expressions of amazement and outpouring of love for Chloe were lovely, one thing Nicole was not expecting was the barrage of criticism directed at her dad, whose work-from-home job had been the catalyst for Chloe's departure from the family. Strangers from all over the world were quick to accuse Mark Bush of heartlessness and irresponsibility for surrendering Chloe in the first place.

Nicole admits she found it very difficult to cope with the abuse aimed at her father. 'I'm just a normal person; I'm not used to having a story like this blow up, so it was hard to get that kind of criticism,' she says. 'At first I was like, "People, you don't know me and you don't know my situation!" These days we would have personally found her a new home, but this was back before social media was part of our lives. We took her to WAHS because it was a no-kill shelter and we knew she would be adopted.'

Mark, however, wasn't fazed by the unsolicited judgement. He did what he felt was right for his family at the time, and Nicole understood even as a child what a difficult choice it was for him to make.

'Dad and I talked about the criticism. I was really upset by it, but he let it go more easily than me. It bothered me more, particularly because it wasn't the end of the world for Chloe. Her story had a happy ending,' she says.

And happiness really was what it was all about after Chloe returned to Nicole. Over the next few months, the Grimes family showered their new old dog with all the love she deserved. She was well and truly elderly, but finding her first owner again gave Chloe Bear a new lease on life.

'The only signs of age that I really noticed were that she didn't have teeth anymore, so we had to give her soft food. That didn't matter – she still scarfed it down.' Nicole laughs. 'I also think she may have been going blind, but she still had a lot of energy. She acted like a puppy.'

They had shared four wonderful years together what felt like a lifetime ago, and Nicole hoped they would have at least that many the second time around.

Tragically, it wasn't to be.

Just after Chloe Bear's eleventh birthday, when she had been back with Nicole for nine months, she died in her sleep.

'Isaiah and I got home from work one night and I went to the bathroom and was washing my make-up off when I heard Isaiah yelling my name. He sounded frantic,' says Nicole. 'He said, "I think Chloe's dead – she's not moving." She was lying there in her bed.'

For Nicole, Chloe's sudden passing was every bit as shocking as her miraculous return. She was devastated, and found herself wracked with guilt that, after everything the little dog had been through, she hadn't somehow been able to give Chloe more time.

'I actually have no idea how she died. I don't know if it was old age or something else. I felt a sense of guilt, like, *Did I do something?*' she says. 'We were in a state of shock. It was just so sad, because it had been so nice to have her back.'

In time, though, the simple fact that she *had* had Chloe back, albeit only for a short time, began to ease the ache of her loss.

'I did take comfort in the time we'd had together again, and it was so nice to have had that opportunity,' Nicole says. 'I felt blessed in that respect.'

She had never forgotten her first dog, a faithful friend who chose Nicole as her favourite. In return, the universe conspired to bring them together again, ensuring that Chloe's life ended in the same place it began: wrapped in the love of her very first human.

Holly

The dog who conquered the outback

Strangers often tell Larry Mitchell that he doesn't look like the sort of bloke who should have a little, fluffy, cream-coloured dog at his heels. He looks like the sort, they say, that would be more likely to have by his side a big, burly German shepherd or Rottweiler.

Larry supposes people say these things because he's big and robust, with the well-worn hands and permanent tan of a man who has spent most of his adult life travelling some of the remotest parts of Australia, camping in the bush for weeks on end and working as a gold prospector.

But Larry doesn't buy into stereotypes. He reckons those unsolicited comments about what breed of dog he 'should' have say more about the people who make them than they do about him. Because, you see, Larry is a bit of a softie at heart. He dotes on his partner, Donnabelle Capoy, and their four-year-old daughter, Samonah.

And he loves little dogs. Always has.

'I've had dogs all my life. We used to have Australian silky terriers when I was a kid. I used to get ripped for it, but I love my little dogs,' he says. 'Small dogs are as intelligent as any other dog – they don't realise they're small! If anyone suspicious is around, they'll still let you know.'

In 2005, Larry met a petite pooch who proved all of that to the nth degree. Her name was Holly, and she was firmly of the belief that a diminutive stature is no barrier to a big attitude – and an even bigger life.

Holly was a maltalier (or a cavamalt, depending on how you like your portmanteaus), which is a cross between a Maltese and a Cavalier King Charles spaniel. Larry adopted her in Victoria when she was about five years old, after her former owner decided Holly no longer fit in with her family.

'Holly was a giveaway, because the young lass that owned her had just had a baby and decided she didn't want the dog anymore,' he says. 'She was a very good looking little dog, very cute. I couldn't understand why the young girl gave her away. I can't see how you could do that, because they become a part of your family.'

Whatever the reason, Holly was now part of Larry's family. And it wasn't long before he got a sense of why she might have exasperated her previous owner.

'Holly was very adventurous. She was an unbelievable escape artist.' He laughs. 'If you put her in the backyard, she'd be in the front yard within an hour. She'd often just go and sit at the neighbours' place. She'd let me know, *I'm not going to go anywhere, I'll just be here.* She didn't want to run away; she just didn't want to be locked up.'

Happily for Holly, in Larry she had found an owner whose wanderlust matched hers. A consummate bushman, he has spent all his working life roaming the bush. He travels in a motorhome that is fully equipped for off-grid camping and also owns a small home on South Australia's Kangaroo Island, where his adult son lives.

Holly positively adored their transient lifestyle. 'I've always worked in the bush, so I've always done a lot of travelling. Holly spent fifteen years out in the bush with me, on and off. She was very adventurous,' says Larry. 'I've always had motorohomes and she'd just sit up the front with me. She'd wander around the motorhomes like she was walking around a house. She just loved people. She loved cars and loved travelling.'

She was a quirky little thing, with a handful of idiosyncrasies that set her apart. 'When she'd run along she'd always lift up one of her back legs, and it was never the same one.' Larry laughs. 'She'd hop along.'

Before Larry met Donnabelle, when it was just him and Holly, they spent a lot of time on Kangaroo Island. His son, Sam, and daughter-in-law, Dana, own the Kangaroo Island Wildlife Park – a kind of utopia for plucky little Holly.

'Holly spent probably five years at the park, on and off. She used to get out at night-time and chase the possums. There's four dingoes at the park and Holly used to walk past them in the evenings as if to say, *Ha-ha, I'm out and you're not,*' he says. 'About five o'clock, she knew it was the time the park closed, so she'd sneak down to the feed room and see what was left over on the floor. She was like a vacuum cleaner.'

She more than held her own in the company of Sam's German shepherd, Rikku, who was 25 kilos heavier and a good half a metre taller than her. 'Holly got on well with Rikku. One night they were chasing the possums together and Rikku was scared of them and Holly wasn't,' Larry says. 'She wasn't scared of anything. She'd chase chickens. If another dog had a go at me she'd have a go straight back. She thought she was a Great Dane or something. She was a little terror.'

The daredevil dog also became well known in the wider Kangaroo Island community. 'Occasionally she'd walk down to the nearest township, Parndana, which was about 2 kilometres away. The bus drivers knew her, so they'd stop and give her a ride back to the park.'

That was the remarkable thing about Holly: for all her exploring, she rarely lost her way. She was waylaid a handful of times, but always found her way home to Larry eventually, even when they were travelling and camped in a new or unfamiliar spot – albeit sometimes via a more circuitous route than she might have intended.

It was like she'd been fitted with a homing beacon. While she liked to sniff out her surrounds, she never allowed Larry to be out of her sight for long. For fourteen years, they never spent a day apart.

'She never got lost. She had a bush sense. Even when I

was prospecting, she could be a hundred metres away and then a moment later she'd be right by my side.'

Even as she aged, Holly never gave Larry much cause for concern. By early 2019, she was an impressive eighteen years of age and was getting a little stiff, but she was still often mistaken for a puppy. Knowing her as he did, Larry was really the only one who could see that she was starting to slow down.

'Physically she didn't look much different. She could still jump down out of the motorhome, albeit a little bit gingerly. It was just the way she walked – you could tell she was an old dog. But you could also tell she was happy. When she wanted to play, we'd see the young Holly trying to come through,' he says. 'She had to have her teeth all cleaned up and she lost her hearing a little bit, but once she saw me she'd be fine. She could still see with no trouble.'

It certainly never entered his head to trade Holly in for a younger model the way some people do when their dogs get old. 'To me it's like, because your grandmother is old, are you going to throw her out? It's no different. An old dog is no different to a younger one,' he says. He couldn't fathom how anyone could abandon a senior pooch after a lifetime of love. 'They get a little bit slower, but they're so faithful. They've given you so much love and attention.'

But the summer of 2019 brought with it a close call for Holly. That February, Larry, Donnabelle and Samonah were en route to Kalgoorlie and the Western Australian gold-fields, together with Holly and their other dog, three-year-old Sasha, a Maltese–Shih tzu cross.

The family decided to break up their journey near the small city of Port Augusta, in South Australia, setting up camp for the night off the Eyre Highway. While the humans turned in for the night, Holly and Sasha curled up outside the motorhome, self-appointed 'nightwatchdogs'.

Around two o'clock in the morning, Larry's phone rang. The caller asked if his dog was missing. Knowing that both Holly and Sasha had been asleep by the door just a couple of hours earlier, and that neither dog was likely to wander far, he blearily replied that he was confident his pets were safe and sound.

But the caller was insistent: he was sure he had Larry's dog in his care.

'Holly had my son's phone number on her collar, and this gentleman had rung my son and then rung me,' he recalls. 'Turns out she'd wandered onto the highway and a truck driver had picked her up. He'd taken her a hundred kilometres up the road, so at three o'clock in the morning I had to drive to Whyalla and pick her up.'

It was hard to be too annoyed about the early wake-up call – when Larry arrived, Holly was very pleased with her little sojourn. 'Any time I had to fetch her from somewhere she shouldn't have been, she just wagged her tail and had her tongue hanging out, a happy look on her face,' he says. Her decision to take a ride with the truck driver was entirely unsurprising. 'She loved everyone, it didn't matter who.'

With Holly safely back in the motorhome, the whole clan continued on to WA and what they hoped would be an incident-free few weeks of gainful prospecting. But if Larry thought that Holly's midnight misadventure had taught her a lesson about straying too far from camp, he was in for a shock.

In late March, elderly Holly went walkabout again. This time in the vast, empty goldfields around Kalgoorlie. In the blistering heat of an early autumn that still felt like high summer.

And this time there was no 3 a.m. phone call. There was no mad dash to collect an elated and unapologetic dog.

This time, Holly was gone.

The inland city of Kalgoorlie-Boulder, known simply as Kalgoorlie, lies 600 kilometres east-northeast of Perth. It's a town of contrasts. In the late nineteenth and early twentieth centuries, the Gold Rush brought some 200,000 mostly white prospectors to the town, where they lived alongside the area's Indigenous population. Flimsy miners' huts and stately Victorian buildings – many of which served as pubs – dotted the flat desert landscape; the cool interiors of the latter provided some respite from the searing summer heat.

Back in the day, Kalgoorlie was infamous as a sort of 'wild west' frontier town. Brawling and carousing were the pastimes of choice for many of its ragtag residents. Men outnumbered women three to one, and bandits and ladies of the night plied their trade alongside ever-hopeful goldminers. It was – and to a certain extent remains – an unpretentious, rough-and-tumble sort of place.

In modern times, Kalgoorlie has produced a diverse group of notable citizens including bawdy comedian Kevin Bloody Wilson and his daughter, singer-songwriter Jenny Talia (aka country musician T.J. Dennis); musician Tim Rogers of You Am I fame; and Nobel Prize–winning microbiologist Professor Barry Marshall.

Kalgoorlie was founded by three prospectors who happened upon a gold deposit in the winter of 1893, and one thing has remained constant since that time: the town's fortunes have always been inextricably linked to the earth. The mining of gold, along with other metals, has always been a major industry in the city. Mining still employs about a quarter of Kalgoorlie's workforce and generates a significant proportion of its income. The concentrated area of large gold mines surrounding the original 1893 find, often referred to as the Golden Mile, has been called the world's richest square mile.

In 2020, Larry and his family bought a home in Kalgoorlie; it's the first time he has been something like a permanent resident anywhere in about as long as he can remember. A regular visitor to the area for decades, he has a number of gold prospecting leases around town. He's had some good finds, as well as times when the ground has yielded nothing much at all.

But whether his prospecting has been fruitful or frustrating, Larry has always loved the stark beauty and harsh tranquility of this part of the world. He has a deep respect for the landscape, too. You've got to – out there neither the heat, the wildlife, nor the vast emptiness will suffer fools.

Larry puts it best: 'There's a whole lot of nothing out there around Kalgoorlie,' he says.

Holly shared Larry's sense of awe. That 'bush sense' he saw in her meant he didn't have to worry too much about her when they were out there together, searching for gold. She had never put a foot wrong, aside from that 'blip' at Port Augusta. After fifteen years by his side, he knew she was more than capable of holding her own.

Which is why it was even more shocking when Holly simply vanished. One moment she was there, the next she just wasn't.

To this day, Larry isn't quite sure how or when his elderly canine companion disappeared. He was camped with Donnabelle and Samonah at the Kalgoorlie International Speedway, about 7 kilometres from the centre of town, on the Goldfields Highway.

Holly and Sasha were 'just hanging out' by the motorhome, lazing about in the shade as the temperature soared past 35 degrees. But the next time Larry checked, Holly was nowhere to be seen.

At first he wasn't especially concerned. Holly would mosey on back in her own time. As the hours passed, however, the fear crept in.

So Larry started walking, tramping through the bush around the campsite. There was no trace of Holly; it was as if she had never been there at all. But Larry was determined. For four long, sweltering days, he scoured the area on foot. When that didn't deliver his beloved companion, he took to the roads, driving further afield in case Holly's little legs had managed to carry her beyond the immediate surrounds.

Larry and Donnabelle also posted appeals for information about Holly's whereabouts on local Facebook pages, in case somebody had picked her up. It didn't seem a likely scenario, though. Holly was microchipped and Larry's son's phone number was embroidered on her collar; surely if she'd been found by a human, he would have heard by now.

Still there was no sign of her. It was as if she had simply dissolved into thin air.

Larry is an optimist at heart – as a professional gold prospector, it's a requirement – and he wanted to believe that his fearless mutt could withstand anything nature threw at her. She had attitude in spades, and had demonstrated time and time again that nothing fazed her.

But as each new day dawned without Holly, he became increasingly distraught. She was a tiny dog lost in an endless, inhospitable wilderness. He was also worried about the local wildlife. Larry had often spotted wedge-tailed eagles hiding under the motorhome. Foxes, dingoes and wild dogs were also common in the area. Any one of those creatures would see Holly as a tasty snack.

It was no way for his faithful old girl to go. 'My main concern was that an animal had got her. I really thought that an eagle or a dingo would've got hold of her.'

And there was the not insignificant fact that she was getting on for twenty years old; how could she possibly survive out there? She was hard of hearing: what if she was nearby but simply couldn't hear Larry calling?

'I'd spent four days just walking the bush. I'd driven everywhere and there was not a sign of her. I thought, *That's it – she's gone,*' he says. 'I feared the worst because it was so hot – about 35 degrees every day. I thought for sure she'd perished with no water or food. I'd given up all hope.'

Mostly, though, it was the mystery of it that preyed on his mind. After fifteen years together, it drove him crazy that he might never see Holly again or know what had become of her. She should have spent her remaining time snoozing in the motorhome and harassing Sasha, not alone in the WA bush, at the mercy of the elements.

'It was the not knowing that was the worst. The thought of her suffering upset me even more than her being missing – the idea that she was lying out there on a 35-degree day, not being able to do anything,' he says. 'I knew that if she was never found, my brain would never stop wondering.'

Though he wanted to do nothing but keep looking for Holly, eventually Larry had no option but to get back to work. He had a family to feed, after all. With a heavy heart, he packed up the Kalgoorlie campsite and drove 400 kilometres north to check on his prospecting leases at Laverton.

Meanwhile, back in Kalgoorlie, unbeknownst to Larry, an article appeared on the front page of the town's daily newspaper, the *Kalgoorlie Miner*. Its headline read: 'Holly a long way from home'.

It wasn't the first time RSPCA WA general inspector Fiona Brown had come across a dog wandering in the bush outside

Kalgoorlie, but this one was different. For a start, she was old – *really* old. Her microchip suggested she was at least eighteen. And she was in good nick, a little scruffy from her time as a stray, but well fed and clearly well loved.

The microchip also revealed the dog's name was Holly, but that was where the useful information ended. Holly had been chipped in Victoria, and the phone numbers linked to her chip were now disconnected.

She had been picked up at a rest stop on the Goldfields Highway, heading north towards the town of Leonora, and brought back to the Kalgoorlie Veterinary Clinic. From there, she had passed into the care of the RSPCA.

Somebody would be missing Holly, Fiona was sure of it. 'She is an elderly dog and considering her age she is in good condition. A dog does not age that well without receiving a good deal of love and care,' she told the *Kalgoorlie Miner*. 'She was matted and dirty – it appeared she had been lost for at least a few days.'

Holly was living with a foster family while Fiona searched for her owners. 'She has settled in well with her foster family, but she is confused. There is little doubt she would be relieved to go home and spend her autumn years with the owners she knows, loves, and has been loyal to for the past decade.'

Fiona had a hunch that Holly had absconded from those owners while they were travelling through the area. She was worried Holly's family may have given up hope of finding her. 'If her owners are travelling and lost her, they may believe she has passed away,' she told the newspaper. 'Being an older dog, surviving in the outback would be full of danger – baits, wild dogs, eagles, mineshafts, dehydration and exhaustion.'

She couldn't have known how uncannily close to the truth she was.

Still, the fact remained that nobody had come forward to claim Holly, and foster care was only a temporary solution. Reluctantly, Fiona booked Holly onto a flight from Kalgoorlie to Perth, where she would be put up for adoption as part of the RSPCA's seniors program.

But she just couldn't shake the feeling that the sweet Maltese cross *did* have owners out there somewhere. 'She wasn't acting like a dog that was lost, she was acting like a dog that was waiting for someone – so we cancelled the flight,' Fiona told the *Kalgoorlie Miner*.

She kept searching. Finally, she discovered a faint phone number embroidered on Holly's collar that had been obscured by her matted fur. Mercifully, this number was not disconnected; Fiona's call was answered by Sam Mitchell, 2300 kilometres away on Kangaroo Island.

Up in Laverton, Larry and Donnabelle were also still searching. Whenever they had enough phone reception out in the bush, they scoured social media and animal rescue websites for any hint of their adored dog. The one source they hadn't thought to monitor was the *Kalgoorlie Miner*, so they had no idea that Holly had made front-page news.

But more than a week after Holly's disappearance, Larry finally got a break.

'Eight or nine days later, Donna said, "Look! Someone's put a picture of her on Facebook."' A Kalgoorlie local had indeed shared Holly's story online. Larry could hardly believe his eyes when he saw her. 'The moment I saw that picture on Facebook it brought tears to my eyes. Just knowing she was alive was like, *Oh my God!* I was so happy.'

Before he had a chance to contact the RSPCA, Larry received a call from Fiona Brown. His son, Sam, had passed on Larry's number. 'They said she was found at the first parking bay on the way out of town, which was 5 or 6 kilometres from where we were camped. That was four or five days after she went missing,' he says. 'So there's about a week where I don't know what happened to her. Whether someone had picked her up and she got out . . . even the RSPCA don't know.'

Larry was ready to jump in the motorhome that very second and race back to Kalgoorlie, but there was official business to complete first. 'They wanted proof that she was ours, so I had to describe different features,' he explains. 'It took about four days before we were reunited.' In total, Holly and Larry had been apart for close to three weeks.

Finally, the day arrived. Larry, Donnabelle and Samonah made their way back to Kalgoorlie. The anticipation was enormous – Larry says it felt like meeting Holly for the very first time. 'It felt like when you go to pick up a brand new puppy. It was similar to that. I was so excited just to have her back.'

Young Samonah was equally thrilled by her playmate's return. 'She kept saying, "Where has she been? Did she go on holiday?" Larry laughs.

Even Sasha, Holly's junior counterpart, was happy to see her (although she had made the most of her absence by eating as much as possible). 'Sasha's not quite like Holly – she's a different personality,' says Larry. 'Holly was always the boss, especially when it came to food. She had to have hers first, and Sasha wasn't allowed to eat until Holly was full.'

When at last he clapped eyes on Holly, Larry admits that tears threatened once more. She was in surprisingly good condition – she had been a little dehydrated, understandably, and a longstanding cyst on her back had ruptured, but she was otherwise no worse for her unplanned desert adventure.

The reunion again saw Holly splashed across the front page of the *Kalgoorlie Miner*, this time with an ecstatic Larry, Donnabelle and Samonah by her side.

'She got pampered a lot for the next few days. I wouldn't let her out of my sight,' he says. 'I never thought I'd end up on the front page of a newspaper over a dog!'

Soon enough, the family was back on the road and life returned to normal. Holly continued to live it up in the motorhome, play with Sasha, dominate mealtimes, and hide under the table when toddler Samonah's affections became a little overwhelming.

*

Not long after her rescue from the bush, Holly turned nineteen. Everywhere she and Larry went, everyone they met was astonished by her longevity. Truth be told, Larry was starting to feel a little astonished himself. 'I think there were about three years where I was thinking she'd go any day, but she always surprised me. She always had that smiley face. She was still a good eater.'

Then, seven months after her outback jaunt, in November 2019, Holly went to sleep one night and simply didn't wake up. She passed away peacefully after almost two decades of fun.

For Larry, it felt like a fitting end for a bold and beloved dog who was always ready for adventure, just so long as she had her human to come home to – wherever that home might have been.

'She's the oldest dog I've ever had. She just kept going and going like a faithful car,' he says. 'I think of Holly all the time.'

Larry had faith that Holly would always return to him, no matter where her explorer's nose led her. Perhaps that faith was the secret to Holly's long life. Because Holly, in turn, had faith in him. He was her companion just as much as she was his. She believed he would do right by her, always, and so she did right by him.

Arnie

The dog who inspired an artist

On the face of it, the calamitous life of Arnie the toy poodle is exactly the type of tale that leads some people to believe that old dogs aren't worth the trouble. Lurching from one disaster to the next, Arnie's long life was littered with enough drama, near-death experiences, and expensive medical problems to fill a book. (Literally: his owner published a book about him.)

Why bother adopting a senior dog, some people might wonder, and risk having to take on all that? Who would sign up for that kind of baggage?

Renowned artist Jane Canfield would, for one. Because Jane understands that Arnie's story isn't about turmoil and catastrophe at all. While Arnie had more than his fair share of challenges, certainly, his story is about loyalty, adventure and art.

Above all, it's about love.

Arnie came into Jane's life in 2005, but she had been a confirmed 'poodle person' for twenty-five years by then. She fell in love with her first toy poodle when she was a teenager.

'My dad had been quite ill, on and off, and he was eventually diagnosed with multiple sclerosis when I was fourteen. I'm an only child, and not having any siblings and Dad being so sick, I asked my parents, "Can I have a dog?"' Jane says. 'Mum being Mum, she said, "Yes – but I'm going to decide what dog it is."'

The dog she chose was a black toy poodle puppy. The family named her Misha, after the 1980 Moscow Olympics mascot Misha the bear, but the little pooch was more commonly called by her nickname, Mish the Dish.

Jane was instantly smitten. 'I adored that little dog. I just latched onto her. I remember thinking, *I'd die if anything happened to her.* There was just such an intense feeling.'

Later, when Jane moved out of home and embarked on her first career, as a graphic designer, Misha stayed with her parents and Jane didn't have a dog for several years. 'Dogless' was a state of being she found she did not enjoy, so when she bought a home at Wentworth Falls, in the NSW Blue Mountains, Jane knew she needed a four-legged friend.

'The house had a big fenced yard and it just clicked. I thought, *Now's the time to get a dog.* I wanted to rescue, so I rang the RSPCA shelter in Katoomba and I just asked them, "Is there anything with poodle in it?" As luck would have it they said, "Yes, there's a chocolate miniature poodle."'

The little dog's name was Goodbye Mr Chips, or Chippy for short, and he had a sad backstory. Katoomba RSPCA also provides boarding services, and two-year-old Chippy had spent three months waiting for owners that apparently weren't coming back for him.

'I went up to the shelter and as soon as I saw him it was love at first sight. I adored him. He was absolutely beautiful,' says Jane.

But just a week later, Chippy's former owners resurfaced, wanting him back. Thankfully, Jane's adoption of him was airtight; there was no way her new best friend could be taken from her. Besides, shelter staff had got to know Chippy well during his unexpectedly extended stay with them and knew he was better off with Jane.

They had been a tight-knit team for almost ten years when, in 2005, Chippy's groomer, Thea, uttered the fateful words: 'You don't want another one, do you?' She knew of a toy poodle who needed a home and thought Jane could be a perfect fit.

Until that moment Jane had never thought about getting a second dog, but she couldn't help but feel moved by the story Thea recounted.

The poodle was at the RSPCA's Yagoona shelter, in Sydney's western suburbs, having been pulled out of a local dog pound by an RSPCA investigator who was fond of the breed.

'He was in the RSPCA system but this inspector used to take him home with her because she didn't want to leave him at the kennels all the time,' says Jane. 'She was fostering him, but she couldn't keep him because she already had several dogs.'

The kind-hearted inspector brought the dog to the Blue Mountains to meet Jane, and once again 'it was instant love'.

His name, according to his microchip, was Armani. He was every bit as good-looking as his fashionable name suggested. 'He was the most beautiful colour — a true silver,' Jane says.

At nine years of age, Armani was already a senior. He wound up in the pound as a stray after he was found wandering the streets of Blacktown in western Sydney. He was awfully thin and lost even more weight at the pound, where he shared a kennel with two bossy Maltese dogs that snatched his food.

Nobody came looking for Armani and, though he was microchipped, his owners could not be located.

'His chip was not kept up to date. The RSPCA went to the address where he was registered and no one there knew of him,' Jane says. Convinced someone must be missing him, possibly an elderly person, she even contacted several aged care homes in the area. 'He was obviously a loved little dog and I knew how distraught someone must be at losing him.'

But when her investigations proved fruitless, Jane was secretly relieved. She had fallen head over heels for the spry senior poodle and was glad he would become a permanent family member, albeit with one major change.

'I couldn't deal with the "Armani" thing so I changed his name to Arnie.' She laughs. 'He was a real little man. He was sturdy and tough and he always smiled. He had a really curved up little face and was always happy.'

Jane, Arnie and Chippy lived in their blissful bubble for the next eight months. Then, out of the blue, Arnie started crying out every time he ate.

Jane immediately whisked him off to the local vet, who suspected Arnie might have infected teeth. He had a dental procedure in which a couple of teeth were removed – but it didn't solve the problem. He was still in pain at every mealtime.

Off he went to a specialist vet hospital in Sydney. There, a CT scan showed a mass inside Arnie's left ear. It was a nasty infection that had never been treated and was now destroying his ear canal.

'The poor little man, it turned out he had to have his ear canal removed. So afterwards he was deaf in that ear,' says Jane. 'The vet said he'd probably had a really bad headache for a long, long time.'

It's testament to Arnie's stoicism and enduringly happy nature that he had been his usual cheerful self even as the infection worsened, right up until the pain became unbearable. Jane couldn't have anticipated at the time just how important that easygoing temperament would be for Arnie in the years to come.

It took the poodle a little while to regain his sea legs after his surgery. The removal of Arnie's ear canal left him slightly unsteady on his feet, and he took to tilting his head permanently to one side. But, as was his way, he simply got on with things.

Soon after, Jane was commissioned to create a painting of a home at Blackheath, in the upper Blue Mountains. Arnie always loved being in the great outdoors, so Jane didn't think twice about taking both Arnie and Chippy with her to reconnoitre the property. It had beautifully manicured gardens and a small dam, which the dogs raced off to explore while Jane turned her artist's eye to the landscape and the light.

'I saw them go over the embankment and then I saw this little ring of ripples in the dam. I didn't think anything of it. Then Chippy came back – no Arnie. I sauntered down there, so it was probably a minute or two after I saw the ripples, and I couldn't see him.'

Jane's first thought was that Arnie must have made his way back to the car, but if that was the case she would have seen him trot past her. Confused, she investigated further. What she saw next made her blood run cold.

'As I stepped forward there was some grass, and at the foot of the grass was what at first looked like weeds. It was Arnie. Because his balance was a bit off, he'd fallen in the dam,' she says. 'He had stopped breathing.'

Jane snatched Arnie out of the water, held him upside down, and vigorously rubbed his little body. Then, acting on 'pure instinct', she started mouth-to-muzzle resuscitation. 'I put my mouth over his muzzle and gave a little puff, because his lungs were so tiny. It wasn't like the movies – no water came out – but he burped. I did it again and he started breathing,' she says.

'I did the whole screaming in the car on the way to the vet thing. If there had been any police around I would have been in trouble. Arnie was semi-conscious at this stage, but the vet said I must have just caught him before his heart stopped.'

Arnie bounced back in no time, but if Jane expected a reprieve from his run of bad luck, she was about to be disappointed. Not long after his brush with death, Arnie started rubbing at his eyes, so much so that he developed ulcers. Back to the vet he went, and the anti-ulcer antibiotic he was prescribed did the job. But as soon as Archie had finished one course of the medication, the ulcers returned.

What nobody realised was that pressure was building inside his left eyeball. Arnie had glaucoma, an eye disease in which the optic nerve that connects the eye to the brain is damaged, usually due to high fluid pressure in the eye. The condition often has no symptoms other than gradual vision loss, which, of course, Arnie couldn't tell anybody about.

By the time the true cause of his ulcers was established, it was too late. Arnie was blind in his left eye. It was later removed altogether, to alleviate his pain and discomfort. He also had glaucoma in his right eye, but Jane was able to manage it with medicated eye drops.

Jane couldn't quite believe how much life had thrown at her sweet old dog in less than a year. While she was sad that he was partially deaf and blind, surely the universe would now take pity on poor Arnie. It could only be smooth sailing from here on in. Right?

'I remember the vet saying, "That's all the disasters – he's had them all now, they can get no worse,"' Jane recalls.

If only that were true.

*

It's hard to say when somebody 'becomes' an artist. For people like Jane, art has always been there, as much a part of her as her own flesh and blood. She's been drawing, painting and creating all her life; her father, Tony Canfield, was also an artist, as were two of her uncles.

She garnered attention for her strong linocut prints while still working as a graphic designer, but it wasn't until her dad passed away in 2004 that Jane became a full-time artist. Her uniquely tonal contemporary paintings, which often depict the landscape of the Blue Mountains and western NSW, have since been shown in dozens of solo and group exhibitions around Australia. She has also won or been highly commended in a raft of prestigious art awards, including winning the 2008 BMAN Crockett Prize.

It's not surprising, given she is frequently inspired by her surroundings, that Jane's dogs often appear in her work. She paints both in her studio and outdoors – known as '*en plein air*' – travelling in her 1974 VW Kombi, 'Dot', always with her canine companions in tow.

'Chippy used to appear in my paintings sometimes, and I used to get commissions for other people's dogs. But Arnie was the one that kept popping up. He still does, occasionally,' she says. 'There'll be a little silver shape. He was like a little silver ghost.'

It was on a painting jaunt to Sydney's northern beaches in 2010 that a by then fourteen-year-old Arnie ran into trouble once again, although that didn't become apparent until five days after they returned home.

'At one in the morning, Arnie had what looked like a neurological episode. He was very wobbly on his feet. I rang the vet in the middle of the night and he said, "It sounds like he's had a stroke – bring him in at eight in the morning,"' she says. 'I had an awful night waiting, but as it got light I took him out so he could go to the toilet and in the daylight I could see this thing under his eye. It hit me what it was: a paralysis tick.'

Suddenly, Jane remembered seeing Arnie sniffing in a patch of long grass during their time by the beach. 'The dogs didn't go into the bush or anything – we were just walking around the streets and the foreshore – but I'm sure that's when it got him.'

Paralysis ticks, which are widespread on the east coast of Australia, commonly attach to dogs and cats. They inject a poison into the animal as they feed, causing weakness, irritation, a change in pitch in the meow or bark, wobbliness and excessive panting. If undiscovered or untreated, ticks can cause severe paralysis and even death.

Jane called the vet again and was instructed to bring Arnie in right away. The engorged tick was removed, but the paralysis had progressed to such a degree that Arnie couldn't breathe on his own and had to be placed on a ventilator.

Jane was wracked with guilt, chastising herself for not acting sooner. 'The day that Arnie fell ill, he had stumbled. I laughed at the time because I thought, *Oh, you're just being silly*. It turns out his back legs were going from the paralysis,' she says. 'He also had this lump under his remaining eye, and I'd seen it but I thought it was just a bit of sleep. I'd tried to get it off and he wouldn't let me, so I just left it. To think we nearly lost him again.'

Thankfully, the plucky poodle recovered from this ordeal too, but a mere two weeks later another catastrophe struck. Arnie and Chippy slept on Jane's bed, and always followed her when she got up. One night, however, Arnie didn't.

'He was standing on the bed sort of moving his head from side to side as if he couldn't see. I just remember thinking, *Oh no, not the other eye.*'

Jane rushed him back to the specialist vet in Sydney, where Arnie was diagnosed with Sudden Acquired Retinal Degeneration Syndrome (SARDS). He had indeed gone blind in his remaining eye. SARDS has no known cause, though Jane is convinced it was brought on by the tick bite just a fortnight earlier, since tick-borne diseases are associated with several eye problems, especially in dogs. Arnie's right eye was ultimately also removed.

Even without his eyes, Arnie's lust for life remained undimmed. 'He was such a happy little man. It was rare that I would see him sad,' Jane says.

Some of her favourite photographs of her joyful companion were taken at a beach in northern NSW. 'I worked out that he adored the beach. I've got these beautiful pictures of Arnie in his harness on the beach, running like the wind. He knew he was safe because he couldn't run into anything on the beach,' she says.

'I had him on a lead and he was running through the water, tearing around, so happy. His little face was all lit up.

It was amazing that, even with no eyes, you could still see the expressions on his face.'

At home, Jane made adjustments to her daily life to accommodate Arnie's new reality. She bought a playpen so he could be safe and secure in the house when she was concentrating on painting.

He would fret when left alone, so she took him everywhere, carrying him in a sling so he could feel her next to him.

'Psychologists would have had a field day with me! He came to parties. I smuggled him into the movies in a backpack or a little bag and he'd sit beside me or on my lap. I remember once staying at a hotel in the middle of Sydney where dogs weren't allowed. I had him in a basket with just a shawl over the top and I'd take him downstairs to go to the loo on a patch of grass out the front. It was so obvious – sometimes the basket would be wobbling a bit – but I'd just walk confidently and nobody ever asked me about it.'

If it truly wasn't possible to bring Arnie somewhere, rather than leaving him alone at home, Jane would set up a corral for him in her car, always making sure that he had water and was cool or warm enough.

But on one memorable night, Arnie decided he no longer supported this plan.

'I was at a restaurant and he was asleep on the front seat of the car. He must have woken up, because he just started howling. This man came into the restaurant threatening to call the police,' Jane says. 'After that, if I had to leave him in the car for long I'd put a note on the door saying,

Thank you for caring, but I'm fine. I'm blind and if I'm howling it's not for long – Mum's not far away.'

In 2008, Jane's beloved chocolate brown poodle, Chippy, had died at the age of thirteen. Sadly, Chippy had never really warmed to his adopted brother. While he tolerated the new arrival at first, he grew increasingly jealous as Arnie battled his various health problems and required more care from Jane. Chippy attacked Arnie on more than one occasion and Jane eventually had to keep them separated when travelling in the car.

'Chip loved me, and he was jealous because he saw that Arnie was getting more attention. I adored them both but naturally, because Arnie was, I suppose, like a child with special needs, we were closer and the bond was getting stronger and stronger,' she says. 'Chip must have felt like a second-class citizen.'

After Chippy passed away, Jane had decided theirs would be a one-dog household for the rest of Arnie's life. She knew her blind, partially deaf little poodle wouldn't cope with another dog joining the family.

So they continued to have adventures, just the two of them, for the next decade. Arnie accompanied Jane on her camping trips and *en plein air* painting sessions, as well as to exhibition openings, art fairs and just about every-where else.

He became so well known among Jane's circle of friends, and even her art buyers, that her long-time friend Sophie Potter Seeger, an artist and interior designer, decided he should have his life story told in a book.

'So many people had met him through my studio and at galleries. He had a real following. He was probably the famous one in the family,' says Jane.

Sophie wrote the story while Jane, of course, provided the pictures, and *Arnie: The Artist's Muse* was self-published in 2013. Arnie had reached an incredible seventeen years of age, and was to be feted at a glittering book launch.

Instead, the book would be his bittersweet swan song.

When Arnie lost his sight, he became adept at using his other senses to navigate his way through the world, particularly his powerful sense of smell. Nevertheless, Jane was always conscious of things like rearranging the furniture in her cottage; she didn't want to do anything that might cause Arnie to feel unsafe in his environment.

This was easier said than done in her studio, where canvases of all shapes and sizes were constantly coming and going and being moved around. His playpen was one defence against this shifting terrain, but sometimes Arnie would still manage to follow his nose straight into trouble.

On one occasion, in 2012, Jane was engrossed in her work and didn't see Arnie leave his bed. He bumped into a wall and knocked over a painting, which fell and struck him on the head. The blow caused Arnie to have a seizure.

Once again, Jane rushed Arnie to the vet. The seizure abated and the vet confirmed that it had probably been caused by the bump on the head.

He remained seizure free until the following year, when he and Jane were house-sitting for friends. They had been out for the day and when they returned, Jane put Arnie in the garden, which he knew well, while she made a phone call.

'After about a minute I walked outside and there was Arnie, lying on his side, having an awful seizure. It wouldn't stop,' she says. 'I raced him up to the vet clinic and they kept pumping him full of stuff, but they couldn't get it to stop either.'

Finally, the vet had to deliver the devastating news: he had administered the maximum amount of medication, but he simply couldn't control the seizure. Even if Arnie did manage to come out of it, he would certainly have severe brain damage.

And so, after twelve years together, Jane let her best friend go. It was 19 September 2013; Arnie had turned seventeen just two months earlier.

Jane was utterly heartbroken by Arnie's death. 'It would have been devastating regardless – I always knew it was going to be an awful time – but seeing someone you love seizuring like that is just so horrible.'

She wasn't quite ready to say goodbye to the brave poodle who had been through so much – and had given so much – so she kept him with her for the next couple of days. It was, she says, a crucial part of accepting that Arnie was gone.

'When someone dies, the way we are today we tend to not spend time with them. In the past we would have had to prepare the body for burial, and it's now coming out that this is beneficial for our human psyche,' Jane explains. 'It was the same with Arnie. When he died, I kept him with me that night. I was so used to him sleeping with me, so he slept on the pillow beside me. It might sound a bit creepy to some, but the next day I carried him around in my sling. I had that time with him, which I found was so important.'

When the time came to lay Arnie to rest, Jane's friends rallied around her.

'My friends were amazing. One made a hardwood coffin for him with brass fixtures, and I got a little plaque made for the top. Mum made him a beautiful little green cushion with a blanket,' she says.

'I drove him home and there were all my friends in the garden. One was playing guitar. People had brought food. There were flowers. A gardening friend had found the site and said, "We've bought a tree to plant. Let's create a beautiful garden for him." We sprinkled liver treats in the hole where we placed Arnie's casket. We had a proper wake for him.'

It was the perfect send-off for a dog that had lived a long and truly extraordinary life. The book launch, which was held two weeks later, was an equally joyous celebration of Arnie's colourful existence, though Jane still can't bring herself to read the book.

When Jane later sold her home and moved fifteen kilometres east to a crumbling 1850s inn at Lidsdale, which she is restoring with her partner, Creese, she brought Arnie with her and had him reinterred at her new home.

Even today, Jane finds herself reflecting often on Arnie's life and what he meant to her – and he does still appear in her paintings. She marvels at the fact that in spite of all the stress and ill health he endured in his life, he never lost his spirit, his inner wellspring of happiness.

'Arnie was just amazing. It sounds like his life was really sad, but it wasn't. There were so many laugh-out-loud moments, and he brought so much joy. He was the happiest little dog, and he stayed such a happy little dog. He didn't lead a boring life. He was a fighter,' Jane says.

'Sometimes I worry: was it just because he was so needy that I loved him so much? Of course there was that bond that grew, but I adored him from the moment I saw him. We were a team, and it wasn't just me: everyone loved him.'

Jane expected to be without a dog for some time after Arnie died. Her heart needed to heal, and she thought that meant she shouldn't risk becoming attached to another four-legged friend.

But five weeks later, she found herself driving to the south coast to meet a three-year-old poodle called Molly whose elderly owners needed to rehome her. 'I was going to be dogless for a little while, but I have a lovely friend, Lee, who said, "You know, Jane, the best thing you can do is get another dog." He knew someone who knew someone who knew that Molly needed a new home.'

Of course, Jane took Molly home. 'She made me laugh. It fills that little hole, having a dog to look after.'

Two years after that, a different friend told Jane about a shoodle – a Shih tzu–poodle mix – that needed rescue, so she adopted five-year-old Daisy as well. Both poodles have now almost achieved senior status themselves.

Creese also has two dogs, Clare the border collie and Astrid the Swedish Vallhund, so the inn at Lidsdale has its own canine pack these days.

Jane is so grateful to her friends for encouraging her to open her heart to dogs again.

'I thought I would have a longer break than I did when Arnie passed away. I've had people who've lost a senior pet say to me, "I can't get another dog, I'm so heartbroken." But the best thing you can do is get back on that horse,' she says. 'You're not being disloyal to the dog you lost. You're saving another little soul that needs a home. This is what life is about. There are times when sad things happen, but hopefully you have lots of happy times as well.'

That's what Jane really wants people to understand about senior dogs. Yes, they may not be as sprightly as their younger counterparts, but often they're also calmer and more settled. Yes, they may have health issues, but they bear their challenges with a resilience and unwavering happiness that can be a lesson to us all.

The sad things aren't the things that matter. The things that matter are the fun, the laughter, the steadfast loyalty. And the thing that matters most of all is the love.

Puppy

The dog who never grew up

Puppyhood is a time of great exploration. Young dogs are constantly testing the boundaries, trying and pushing the limits of behaviour. Chew this, not that. Pee outside, not inside. Nap in this basket, not on the couch. They're forever tripping over stuff, falling off things, and busily attempting to figure out how the world works. Their entire lives are a wondrous and delightful process of trial and error.

Of course, as they grow into adolescence and then adulthood, most puppies leave those goofy days behind. Dogs never outgrow their silliness entirely – that's why we love them – but generally speaking, they learn from their mistakes.

That's *puppies*, anyway. Not Puppy, though.

Puppy the 70-kilogram Pyrenean Mountain Dog was a giant goofball every day of his life. It's part of the reason why his owner, Karen James, and her family adored him so much. Living in the rural US town of McLeary in the state of Washington, Puppy loved to ramble and follow his nose all over their 6-acre property – and beyond.

It was the 'beyond' part that got him into trouble in the summer of 2018. And again in the summer of 2019. Oh, and that one other time, years earlier.

A lifelong horse lover, Karen is very familiar with large animals and their idiosyncrasies, though the dogs in her life had always been a little more diminutive. As a child she doted on her family's Boston terrier, Tuffy, but her first marriage meant an involuntary moratorium on dog ownership.

'I married a man who was allergic to animals, so for many years I couldn't have a dog,' says Karen, who works as a school nurse.

Eventually, she could no longer tolerate her dogless life and adopted from the local pound an Australian shepherd mix called Teddy, who was to be an outside-only companion, in deference to her then husband's allergies.

'I was going to have a dog whether he liked it or not. I wanted our children, Tommy and Amanda, to have a dog,' Karen explains. 'I think dogs are valuable for children, that relationship they have. The unconditional love that you get from a dog is really valuable in a kid's life.'

When her marriage ended – 'It may have had something to do with the dog!' – Karen, the kids, her horses and Teddy moved to a larger property, an oasis for children and pets alike.

'Behind me is another six-acre property, and behind that

is timberland owned by a timber company,' she says. 'We're talking wilderness back there. There are logging roads and trails – we have four-wheeler bikes and use them for recreation.'

One of Karen's new neighbours was a breeder of Pyrenees Mountain Dogs, which are known in North America as Great Pyrenees (or simply Pyr for short). When one of the neighbour's dogs had a litter in 2007, she and Tommy went to visit the pups.

'I said to my son those famous last words: "Would you like to visit the puppies?" Tommy was maybe sixteen and he said, "Are we going to get one?" I said, "No, we're just going to see them,"' she recalls. 'But Great Pyrenees puppies are the cutest little fur balls you've ever seen.'

The James family had acquired two cats along the way, but one was killed by a coyote soon after the move. The loss of their feline friend devastated the family, especially Tommy, who was very attached to their surviving cat, Blackberry.

'Great Pyrenees were bred to protect livestock, so Tommy said, "We can't lose Blackberry too – we have to get one of those dogs.'

By the time Karen approached her neighbour about buying a puppy, there was just one remaining. He was four months old by then and had been the largest pup in the litter. In fact, he was so hefty that he had been dubbed Big Boy.

Karen brought the chunky canine home. 'I got the $800 dog to protect the free barn cat.' She laughs.

The dog was so big, fluffy and bearlike that Tommy named him Kodiak. He was supposed to be called Kody for short, but from day one the entire family only ever referred to him as Puppy. 'That's the irony: he's this big, giant dog called Puppy. We've never once called him Kodiak and neither has anybody else,' Karen says. 'The vet said, "You cannot call a 70-kilogram dog Puppy" and I said, "Actually, I can."'

Karen later remarried, and her husband, Kevin, likes to good-naturedly tease Tommy and Amanda: 'My stepchildren are so lazy they didn't even name their dog.'

Though Puppy's addition to the family wasn't strictly planned, and Karen had never owned a giant breed before, she was familiar with the Great Pyrenees by reputation if nothing else.

The breed originated working alongside shepherds in the Pyrenees mountains between France and Spain. As well as herding, their job was to protect sheep from predators such as wolves. With their thick double coat, they are ideal year-round workers.

A book written by a Spanish friar in 1617 includes one of the earliest descriptions of these hardy and reliable dogs. By the seventeenth century the Great Pyrenees had become the favoured breed of the French aristocracy, including King Louis XIV's son Louis the Grand Dauphin. A Massachusetts couple, Mary and Francis Crane, established the breed in America in the 1930s.

In their traditional role in the mountains of Europe, Pyrs are naturally nocturnal, and aggressive with any predators that threaten their flock. But that same guardian instinct also means they're generally trustworthy around other animals, especially those that are small, young or helpless. They're known to have an affinity with children, too.

So Karen could have been forgiven if she had expected Puppy to be a somewhat sombre, no-nonsense pet – albeit one she could trust implicitly with Teddy, Blackberry and the children. 'Great Pyrenees are by reputation pretty serious, because they've got a job to do. They're not necessarily as affectionate as other dogs are.'

She respected Puppy's natural drive and wouldn't have minded if he hadn't been interested in cuddles and playtime, so long as he kept the coyotes away. But Puppy evidently didn't realise that, according to his pedigree, he was meant to be an aloof workaholic.

'This dog was super affectionate. He wanted to be hugged. He would come up and lean on you. He just was a very affectionate dog,' says Karen. 'People would be intimidated by his size. They'd say, "Is he gentle?" Puppy was a true gentle giant. I had no doubt that he would put himself between me and any predator, but he would not hurt a human being. That protective instinct was there, but not against other people at all.'

Even at the vet, where staff had been so adamant that Puppy needed a name that better reflected his size and bearing, he impressed with his kind and mellow nature.

'I'd take him to the vet for one thing or another. Sometimes they do things that are not comfortable for dogs, but they would always say, "He is such a nice dog – we could do things that he clearly didn't like and he would just accept it,"' she says.

But for all the ways he defied his breed's conventional behaviour, there was one way in which Puppy was a Pyrenean Mountain Dog to a tee: he had a mind of his own.

According to dog intelligence expert Dr Stanley Coren, Pyrs can be slow to learn new commands, slow to obey and more than a little stubborn. From her experience, Karen says that sounds about right.

One day not long after she moved to McCleary, Puppy showed everyone that he liked to do things his own way.

'My husband and a friend were out riding four-wheelers in the timberland area, and Teddy and Puppy followed. The dogs couldn't keep up with the bikes, so they left them out there,' Karen says.

With all the time the dogs had spent sniffing around in those woods, Kevin and his friend figured they'd easily find their way back home. Teddy did – Puppy didn't.

'They went out there searching for him and found him miles from where they'd last seen him. When our friend rode up to him, Puppy was just standing in the middle of the road, looking terrified,' she says. 'After that I always made sure the dogs were locked up at home when everybody went out on the four-wheelers or the horses. I didn't want to deal with him getting lost again.'

What Karen hadn't anticipated was that Puppy's first solo sojourn in the woods had stirred something in him.

Sure, it may not have gone entirely to plan, but now he had a thirst for adventure.

He wanted more.

Thursday 19 July 2018 was to be a red-letter day for Karen. Her daughter, Amanda, had long since grown up and moved to Texas, but she was back in McCleary for a visit. Amanda had inherited her mother's love of horses, and Karen knew she would want to go riding. She was looking forward to ambling along the picturesque trails on horseback and catching up with her girl.

Puppy, who was eleven years old by then and becoming hard of hearing, desperately wanted to go with them. He made his wishes clear. Since his brief disappearance in the woods, however, Karen was adamant he was not allowed out on the trails with her.

'I often ride with my neighbour, whose Labrador goes on all our rides with us. She always stays close, and it's never been a problem,' she says. 'Puppy always wanted to go, but it was very hot and with his size and height, and how furry he is, I didn't think it was a good idea.'

So Karen made sure Puppy was safe at home with her foster son, Trevor, then she and Amanda saddled up and headed for the timbered area they'd come to know so well.

When Puppy suddenly appeared ahead of them on the trail, Karen was surprised, to say the least. 'We got down to the bottom of the trail and there he was.'

Goodness knew how the hulking hound had managed to wriggle his way out and head them off. It was that famed stubborn streak at work again: he hadn't wanted to stay at home, so he simply didn't.

Reluctant to curtail her ride, Karen decided to let Puppy follow along. It was a bright summer's day and she didn't intend to keep the horses out too long in the heat anyway. How much trouble could Puppy be? 'I thought, *We're not going that far or that fast – it'll be okay*,' she says.

For a while, all was well. Karen and Amanda enjoyed the warm afternoon and the dappled sunlight filtering through the tall trees. Puppy trotted happily along behind them, nose to the ground. The horses' hooves crunched along the trail.

After a little while, however, Puppy decided he'd had enough for one day. And, as always, his independent nature meant he didn't wait for permission to head for home.

When she saw him turn back, Karen was relieved. Now she could focus all of her attention on Amanda. 'Puppy turned down a trail that was a shortcut to home. I thought, *He wants to go home – that's fine*.' As long as he stuck to that path, Puppy would be back at the house in no time.

Except he wasn't.

'Amanda and I went the other way, but when we got home, Puppy wasn't there,' says Karen. 'My husband was so mad at me. "You can't leave the dog – he can't find his way home!"'

She knew Kevin was right: Puppy's internal compass was wonky at best. But Karen wasn't too worried. After all, the first time he went AWOL in those woods, they had located the wayward dog relatively easily. She was confident it wouldn't be too hard to track him down.

'Kevin is more of a pessimist and I'm more of an optimist. He was looking at it like, "The dog's doing to die out there in the wilderness." I was more like, "Oh, no, he'll make it home."'

One of the great things about living in a small community is that people are always willing to leap into action when help is needed. Karen put the call out to her neighbours and soon a small army had rallied, with an assortment of four-wheelers and other all-terrain vehicles (ATVs) to help their search.

The party headed out into the fading afternoon light, searching the trails for any sign of Puppy. But as day turned into night, he remained resolutely missing.

It was cold by now. The mercury had soared to 35 degrees during the day, but nights were notoriously chilly in this undulating part of Washington state. It had recently rained heavily, too, so the timberland was damp and muddy underpaw. All Karen could do was hope that Puppy had found a warm, dry place to curl up for the night.

First thing the next morning, Karen headed back to the search area on foot. This time she took several neighbourhood dogs with her. If she couldn't find Puppy herself, she hoped his fellow canines might be able to sniff him out.

'One big problem was that he didn't hear well anymore. We couldn't just call him and expect him to come. We had to search for him by sight,' she explains.

Still, Puppy was nowhere to be found. It was as if he had vanished into thin air. And if he couldn't hear his would-be rescuers, he was unlikely to be able to hear predators like coyotes either.

By now, even Karen's optimism was starting to wear thin. Short of walking the same trails over and over again, what else could she do to find her beloved dog?

That's when Kevin had a brainwave. Well, two brainwaves in fact.

'He had gone off to work but called me later that morning. He's a problem-solver and he was thinking about hiring a drone to fly over and look for the dog,' says Karen.

But while she appreciated Kevin's ingenuity, she wasn't sure a drone would be any more effective than searchers on the ground. 'It's pretty dense brush out there, and I didn't think a drone could have found him.'

So Kevin made another suggestion: what about a tracker?

A tracker? Karen was confused. Weren't dogs usually themselves the trackers?

'Kevin said, "You need to find a tracker" And I said, "I think they do that for lost children, but I don't think they do it for lost animals."' But thank God he did suggest it, because I would not have thought of it.'

Karen relayed Kevin's suggestion to Amanda, who immediately turned to Google. Within seconds, she had pulled up the website for Three Retrievers Lost Pet Rescue. Not long after that, Karen was on the phone to Three Retrievers' founder, Jim Branson.

Jim is based near Seattle, Washington's largest city, and works with his trained search dogs to find lost pets within a 160-kilometre radius of the city. Happily, McCleary is about 120 kilometres from Jim.

He told Karen he would see her at four-thirty the following morning.

Her hapless old dog would have to spend a second night lost in the wilderness. Karen crossed her fingers and hoped there wouldn't be a third.

True to his word, it wasn't even daylight when Jim Branson and his German shepherd dog, Tino, pulled up to Karen's front door on Saturday morning. Once he arrived, he didn't want to waste a moment.

Jim founded Three Retrievers Lost Pet Rescue in 2012, naming it after the three retriever search dogs he had at the time. The original trio has since passed away and Jim now searches for missing dogs and cats with the assistance of Komu the crossbreed, Fozzie the poodle, and Valentino – Tino for short.

Each scent-trailing dog takes about eighteen months to train, and Jim does that all by himself. He and his dogs have been involved in more than 5000 missing dog and cat cases, and Jim has published handbooks on finding lost pets.

So while Jim didn't want to make any promises, if Puppy was still out there, he had the knowledge and experience to find him. But time was of the essence.

Tino himself had been a lost dog of sorts. His pregnant mother was found wandering in the woods and brought to Jim's non-profit dog rescue, Useless Bay Sanctuary, which he founded in 2013. Jim named her Salma, and she gave birth to Tino the very next day.

He had demonstrated a knack for scent trailing early on and had recently completed his training. This would be Tino's first solo rescue mission.

Jim's first task was to ask Karen to find an item that belonged to Puppy; he would use it for Tino's sensitive nose to imprint on Puppy's scent.

'Great Pyrenees are very furry and shed everywhere, so it was no problem finding something with his scent on it,' says Karen. She gave them some fur from Puppy's bed.

Then she, Jim and Tino headed out into the darkness. Jim instructed Karen to lead them to the place she'd last seen Puppy.

That presented a problem. The woods look very different in the dark, and she became disoriented. 'It was just barely daylight. We went out, and because of the lack of light I got a little bit lost out there,' she says. 'It took us about forty-five minutes to find the spot.'

When she did, they were at the head of a trail that ran steeply downhill. Jim knew that the moment he gave Puppy's scent to Tino it was going to be tough to keep up with his determined dog.

Sure enough, once Tino had a whiff of his quarry, it was time to rock and roll.

'Jim put Tino to work and I just followed as best I could.

There was a lot of going down a trail and hitting a dead end and circling back,' says Karen. 'In the summertime we have a lot of blackberry brambles here. There's a lot of brush and places where trees have come down.'

Another thing there was a lot of was mud. It was thick and gooey, and it was *everywhere*.

'We were scrambling around and Tino kept taking us down into this gully. At one point Jim lost his boot because the mud was so deep and sticky,' she says. 'Western Washington is very wet, so this was a place that probably never completely dries out. Tino just kept taking us back down there.'

It was challenging terrain, to say the least. Karen found the going hard enough; she almost couldn't bear to think about how her deaf senior dog would have coped with it.

After almost an hour of searching, and back in the boggy gully once more, Karen felt her hopes of finding Puppy – and finding him in one piece – starting to fade. 'Jim and Tino got ahead of me. I was still following along behind thinking, *We're not going to find him – what are we going to do next?*'

And then Tino barked. In fact, he wouldn't *stop* barking.

'I got a little bit closer and Jim turned to me and said, "We've found Puppy!"' But when she got to where Jim was standing and Tino was still barking, she was confused. She couldn't see Puppy. 'I said, "Where is he? I don't understand!"'

That's because Puppy didn't look like Puppy at all. He was stuck up to his shoulders in a mud-filled pit, and he was covered in the muck from head to toe.

As Jim later told animal website *The Dodo*: 'When we first saw Puppy, it was hard to make sense of what we were seeing because two-thirds of him were submerged in mud. Tino barked at this strange swamp monster for a bit until he realised it was a dog.'

Puppy was entrenched so deeply in the mud that Karen realised he had probably been there for more than forty hours, ever since he first disappeared; every time he'd tried to dig himself out he would have only been sucked further in.

'He couldn't have laid his head down because he would have drowned. He was a needle in a haystack. If it wasn't for Jim and Tino, Puppy would have died in that mud and I never would have known what happened,' she says.

She was also shocked to realise just how close to home Puppy was: only about twenty metres from where she had been searching with the neighbours' dogs on Friday morning.

'Puppy wasn't that far off one of the major trails. When we were out there we walked by that gully probably a dozen times, but he couldn't hear us so he didn't bark.'

There was also a tiny moment of vindication for Karen: 'We were practically in my neighbour's backyard so, contrary to my husband's belief, he would have made it home if he hadn't got stuck!'

Puppy didn't really react when he was finally found. He was clearly exhausted, not to mention soaking wet, and Karen suspects he may have been in shock. Tino, on the other hand, was elated to have made his first 'walk-up find'.

'Tino seemed to understand that he'd done what he was supposed to do and that he was a success,' says Karen. 'He was pretty happy and playful.'

But her own joy at finding her beloved Pyr was tempered by a new worry: how on earth were they going to get Puppy out of that putrid pit? He weighed 70 kilograms when he was completely dry; who knew how much extra weight he was carrying now that he was sodden and caked with mud?

Plus, he was rooted so firmly in the mire that Karen and Jim were worried about injuring his legs if they pulled him out the wrong way.

Jim laid some branches across the mud so that he could approach Puppy safely. Then he slid Tino's leash beneath Puppy's belly and tried to haul him out that way.

When that proved fruitless, Karen pulled out her phone.

'I called my husband and said, "We've found him but he's stuck, and we're going to need some ropes or straps or something." Kevin got on the ATV and headed out to us,' she says. 'He got some furniture moving straps under Puppy, and between Kevin and Jim they were able to hoist him out.'

Puppy was free at last, but he wasn't out of the woods yet – figuratively or literally.

'When he got out, his legs weren't working. I'm sure he'd lost all feeling, like when your leg goes to sleep. He couldn't stand and he couldn't walk,' says Karen. 'I called the vet and they said he would be cold and had probably lost some circulation. They told me to get him home and get him warmed up.'

And therein lay the next problem: how on earth were they going to get their enormous and exhausted dog home when he couldn't take so much as a step? They couldn't carry him, and he wouldn't fit on the ATV.

Adding to the drama was the fact that Trevor, Karen's foster child, was home alone at the time. The morning was marching on, and she was worried about him waking up and finding everybody had disappeared.

Karen needed a plan, and she needed it quickly.

'We have a little trailer for the ATV, so I said to Kevin, "Take me home, get the trailer, then put Puppy in it and take *him* home." Jim and Tino stayed with Puppy, and I went to get on the ATV,' she says. 'That's when Puppy reacted. He started crying, like, *Don't leave me!* That was heartbreaking. This giant dog, crying.'

Kevin duly deposited Karen at the house and then went back out with the trailer for Puppy.

'I've got a video of him driving up with the dog in the wagon. Trevor had been really worried about Puppy, so he ran up saying, "He's here! He's here!" I think Puppy was so excited,' says Karen.

'He was clearly happy to be home, but he really just needed to rest, and that's what he did.'

Once he had slept off his ordeal, Karen took Puppy to the vet for a thorough check-up. Before his unscheduled adventure, he had been having issues with soreness and weakness in his rear end, so the vet dispensed anti-inflammatory medication in case his temporary confinement had worsened his pain.

Aside from that, Puppy made a complete recovery. He

even became a celebrity after a local news channel aired the story of his amazing rescue. Media outlets around the world soon picked up the tale, and Puppy the elderly Pyr went global.

There is a rather incredible sequel to Puppy's story. Nearly a year after his first rescue, in June 2019, the hapless hound went missing again.

It was a Friday morning and Karen had gone to work as usual. When she arrived home that afternoon, Puppy wasn't there to greet her. It was a little unusual, but not too out of the ordinary.

'I fed the horses and did all the things I usually do, and then later that night I was like, *Where's Puppy?*' she says. 'I went next door to ask my neighbour. He said he'd seen Puppy about 9 a.m., but not since then.'

It was so unlike him to leave the property at all, let alone to get himself lost twice within twelve months. 'He didn't usually go far. Because of his job, he'd do a circuit of the property and wander down to the neighbours and check that out, then come right back home.'

This time it was up to Kevin to spearhead the search-and-rescue effort. He rallied the neighbours and, based on Puppy's previous form, they made a particular effort to look in all the nearby ditches and gullies.

'Kevin's an accountant, so he's very methodical. He was drawing quadrants and all sorts, but they didn't find him. That's when I said, "We need to call Jim,"' Karen says.

Just as before, Jim and Tino arrived the next morning. This time, the rescue effort was a lot more straightforward.

'Tino found him within ten minutes. Puppy was literally within sight of the house,' she says. And he was indeed in a ditch. 'He had wandered in to get a drink of water, I'm sure. As he wandered out, the bank got steeper and steeper. He was wet and, with his weak hind end, he just couldn't get out.'

Jim turned to Karen and said, deadpan, 'I think you should invest in a GPS collar for this dog.'

'I said, "I think you're right!" He wanted to not charge us as much, but we wanted to pay the full amount and support him. Although we appreciated the offer of a repeat-customer discount,' she says.

Karen always meant to buy that collar, but in the end she didn't get the chance. On 4 January 2020, she and Kevin were preparing to leave for an overnight trip when she suddenly felt overcome by an ominous mood.

'Kevin asked if I was ready and I said, "You know, I don't feel right – I think you should go without me." I just had this niggling feeling,' she says.

Soon after, she found twelve-year-old Puppy collapsed and in respiratory distress. He was rushed to the vet, but it was too late. Puppy, the gentle, protective, adventurous, directionally challenged Great Pyrenees passed away.

Though he was old and had been in declining health, Puppy's sudden death was a shock for Karen. 'When you have an old dog you know they're on borrowed time, but you're never really ready. My other animals, I've had to make the decision to euthanise, which carries its own burden, but at least you're prepared.

'Everybody loved Puppy. He was just a sweet, sweet dog. He was this gentle, quiet, affectionate presence. He wanted to be right next to you and looking up at you adoringly.'

But even though his bold spirit – and yes, his stubbornness – had occasionally led him into trouble, Karen knew that Puppy had lived a wonderful life. She took comfort in the fact that she had always done right by him.

'The neighbour I got him from kept his dogs in a dog run and walked them on a leash. Puppy had the run of my place. My neighbour once said to me, "That's the life they were meant to lead: out there on patrol, guarding their property,"' says Karen.

'Puppy was living the life a Great Pyrenees is meant to live.'

And shouldn't that be the goal for all of us?

Magnus

The dog with the bucket list

Magnus the greyhound was both young and old when he was adopted by Kristan and Jason Norris in 2013.

At five years of age, Magnus was practically still a puppy when it comes to greyhounds. They typically enjoy much longer lives than many other large dog breeds – on average greyhounds live for twelve to fifteen years.

But as an ex-racing dog, Magnus was already an elderly gentleman. According to Animals Australia, the life expectancy of a racing greyhound is just four-and-a-half years. The animal advocacy group says just 10 per cent of dogs born into the racing industry live out their natural lifespan.

Magnus raced for three years, starting in 2009, when he was eighteen months old. He was successful, too, winning twenty races and finishing in the top three in more than a dozen others. But even with his impressive track record,

Magnus's future looked uncertain once he was retired from racing in mid-2012.

The handsome brindle dog was handed over to a Perth veterinary clinic that had an existing relationship with his trainer. And that's where he stayed. He became the clinic's resident donor dog, providing lifesaving blood donations for sick or injured dogs, and even cats.

When he wasn't doing that, Magnus's world was a small enclosure out the back of the clinic, with only a short daily walk and an occasional weekend sleepover at the home of a veterinary nurse to break up the monotony. While it was better than the alternative – an explosive report aired on ABC's *Four Corners* in 2015 found that the racing industry kills up to 17,000 healthy greyhounds every year – it wasn't much of a life. What Magnus needed was a devoted owner willing to give him the life he deserved.

Kristan and Jason weren't aware of these grim statistics when they started thinking about adopting a dog in 2012. The couple had been together for two years and, having recently moved in together, they felt their new home needed a four-legged addition.

For Kristan, a lifetime of dog ownership was a foregone conclusion. She grew up with dogs and had missed having a canine companion in her twenties, when she felt that her busy work and social life, and living in rented homes, would have made it impossible.

'I had grown up with black Labradors. I guess my mum, having two little kids, figured they were great family dogs. We loved their friendly nature,' she says. 'I always knew

I wanted dogs and assumed that when I grew up I would follow in the same vein and have Labs.'

Jason's formative experiences with dogs were a little different. Born in the United Kingdom, he moved with his family to his dad's home state of Tasmania when he was in high school. The family had a dog, but when Jason later relocated to Western Australia to pursue a job opportunity, the pooch went to a farm.

In the case of Jason's furry friend, 'going to the farm' was not a euphemism. 'He was a working breed, a farm dog,' says Kristan. 'He was really Jason's dog, but Jason was over here in Perth and his family just didn't have time for the dog. He wasn't getting walked enough and he was getting really bored. In the end, one of their family friends took him on and he went to live on a farm.'

Kristan and Jason agreed they wanted to adopt their first dog rather than buy from a breeder. Jason researched Perth-based rescue groups and suggested they pay a weekend visit to a nearby shelter with the shared understanding that if they fell in love with a dog that day, they'd take it home.

Kristan says the excursion was a sobering experience. The vast majority of dogs there were Staffordshire bull terriers or Staffy mixes; the breed is notoriously one of the most surrendered to Australian shelters and pounds, which is ironic considering a purebred puppy can cost upwards of $1500.

'That was heartbreaking. They're all looking at you with these pleading eyes and barking. It just really highlighted to me that you need to choose an appropriate dog for your family,' she says.

The couple didn't fall in love with a dog that day. In fact, they decided to slow down their search so they could be sure they were making the best decision for both themselves and their future pet. 'It requires a lot of thought. We lived in a townhouse and we didn't have a yard. We both had full-time jobs. It was like, "Let's hold our horses and not rush into anything."'

Several months later, Jason presented Kristan with a new idea: what about a greyhound? He had been reading up on the breed and discovered they are extremely low mainte-nance, easygoing dogs. In other words, potentially a perfect match for the couple's lifestyle.

Kristan initially was not convinced. 'I remember my reaction: "A greyhound? What the hell are we going to do with a greyhound?!" I just couldn't imagine how this was going to work,' she says. 'Like most people, my perception was that greyhounds were high maintenance, high-energy dogs. It was not the type of dog we had been talking about.'

She had never even seen a pet greyhound. Her only exposure to the breed had been the occasional evening at the dog track with her grandparents as a child. 'You never saw them around the place. That was all my understanding was: that they were racing dogs.'

But Jason was genuinely excited by the prospect, so Kristan promised to consider it. She went to work the next day and discussed the idea with some colleagues. 'The girl who sits next to me piped up with, "I've got a greyhound – they're amazing!" And off she went. The more she went on about how brilliant they were the more I thought, *Maybe she's onto something here.*'

When she got home that night, she told Jason she was in.

After that, searching online for adoptable greyhounds became their nightly pastime. 'We'd lie in bed and watch YouTube videos of other people's greyhounds. We started to see that they're not just racing dogs – they're fun and silly and they have real personality,' says Kristan.

'We also started to learn more about the rehabilitation of ex-racing dogs. They're in kennels all their lives and have very limited social interactions. We really felt sorry for these dogs and knew we had to adopt one.'

For three or four months, they pored over pictures of gorgeous greyhounds that were looking for their forever homes. And though they wished they could adopt all of them, they were waiting to feel that intangible connection that meant 'this is our dog'.

By Christmas that year, they still hadn't felt that spark, and Kristan felt they should suspend their search until the new year. A recent summer thunderstorm had destroyed part of their back fence, and they were still waiting for their insurance company to send someone to fix it, so at that point they couldn't offer a dog a secure yard anyway.

It was then, of course, that she felt the spark.

A small greyhound-rescue group called Greyhound-Angels of WA shared a picture of a male greyhound on their Facebook page. His name was Magnus and he was living in a vet clinic.

'He was a big, beautiful brindle boy and he had reindeer antlers on. He had the saddest-looking eyes I've ever seen,' Kristan says. 'I swear I saw his photo first and sort of thrust it Jason's way. We were both really interested.'

They were also both really busy, as often happens during the festive season. They didn't have a chance to enquire about Magnus until early 2013. Fortunately for the couple, he was still waiting at the vet – in fact, he'd been waiting for six months.

'I rang the vet and they said we were welcome to come and meet him anytime. So we did – it was a Sunday and we got straight in the car and drove thirty or forty minutes to see him,' she says.

First impressions were mixed. Magnus was undeniably gorgeous. 'He was just beautiful, so big and so regal looking,' says Kristan. But he didn't seem overly interested in her and Jason.

It was a hot, muggy January day, and it was raining, so they weren't able to take him outside for a getting-to-know-you walk. All they could do was sit next to his kennel and dispense a steady stream of treats. 'I can't say he was particularly keen on us. We were nobody to him – just some people feeding him treats.'

Extracting information about Magnus from the clinic's staff proved a frustrating endeavour, too. Kristan had a young niece and wanted to make sure any dog she adopted could cope with small children.

'They said, "We don't know. He's here in a kennel – he doesn't see kids." We asked about little dogs. They said,

"We don't know." I asked about cats and they said, "He's more scared of them than they are of him." No one could tell us anything. It was all a bit strange, and I left there feeling a bit ho-hum about it all.'

They went straight from their meet-and-greet at the vet to a birthday party, and Kristan found herself admitting to her friends that she wasn't sure if Magnus was the right dog for her and Jason after all.

What she didn't know, however, was that Jason was in love. He had fallen for Magnus hook, line and sinker, and he was convinced the big, quiet canine was destined to be theirs.

Kristan went to work on Monday and Tuesday as usual, while Jason stayed home; he's a teacher and it was the summer school holidays. When she arrived home on Tuesday afternoon, he wasn't there. She figured he was at the gym and would be back soon.

Jason did indeed come home soon after, but he didn't have a sweaty gym bag in tow.

He had Magnus.

'My heart just about burst,' says Kristan. The instant she saw the giant greyhound standing in her lounge room, her trepidation about adopting him vanished. She knew Jason was right: he was their dog.

'He was so goofy. He was banging into everything. His tail was swiping things off the coffee table. It was like you see in the movies,' she laughs. 'It hit me: *Oh my god, we have a really big dog in a really small house!*'

There was also the matter of the backyard fence.

'I said, "What about the fence?" and Jason said, "I've patched it up." I went outside and it was sort of barricaded, but it was flimsy. If a rescue group had come and seen it, we would never have passed the inspection,' she says. 'But there were no home checks with Magnus. He cost us $100 and it was the best $100 we've ever spent in our lives.'

Flimsy fences didn't matter. What mattered was that Magnus was home, and Kristan and Jason were going to give him the beautiful life he deserved.

By 2017, Magnus had lived with Kristan and Jason for four years, and they still marvelled every single day at what an utterly perfect dog he was.

'We definitely knew he was something special. We used to talk about it all the time. We'd joke, "Who rescued who here?"' Kristan says. 'Magnus turned our house into a home. We were no longer just a couple – we were a family. He was not just a dog.'

Magnus had impeccable manners. He never had a toileting accident in the house, never jumped up on people or tried to steal food from the kitchen bench. He never even tried to breach the rickety temporary fence that was in place when he first arrived.

He hadn't been trained to be polite. Rather, Kristan felt he was almost institutionalised as a result of his former career as a racing dog. The notion of putting a paw out of line simply never entered his head.

'If he was walking down the hallway and you got a dining chair and put it in front of him, he would just stop walking. Any other dog would try to go over it or push past it,' she says. 'He was such a strong dog – he could have gone straight past it, but it had never occurred to him to question anything. I think he'd just been trained to keep everything in.'

Perhaps that explains why Magnus also rarely barked. Greyhounds are not known to be especially vocal dogs, but he was taciturn in the extreme: Kristan can recall exactly three occasions when Magnus barked, just a single *woof* each time.

Magnus continued to donate blood after he was adopted. In 2015, his donation saved the life of a nine-month-old Newfoundland puppy whose liver had inexplicably ruptured. Kristan later discovered that the 50-kilogram puppy, Harriet, belonged to one of her friends. It was a moment of serendipity that underscored just how fated Magnus's role in their lives seemed to be.

And, of course, in addition to his flawless behaviour, Magnus was absolutely beautiful. 'He was so impressive looking, so muscular. We used to sit there and just marvel at him,' says Kristan. 'You couldn't come up with a better design for speed than this dog. He was this fine specimen, this beast.'

For such a big, robust dog, Magnus was also surprisingly agile.

'He generally had no idea about his size in relation to other things, but once he figured out how long he was, and that *If I stand here I'm going to hit the coffee table*, he was ballerina-light on his feet,' she explains. 'He had such a soft, gentle way of moving through the world. People used to say to us, "How did you train him to be so good?" But we couldn't take credit for it all. He was just a gentleman – that's the word that always comes to mind with Magnus.'

Greyhounds are well-known lounge lizards, and Magnus was no different. He loved lazing about the house and only ever wanted a ten- or twenty-minute daily walk – but he definitely did want it. That inherent laziness may have lulled Kristan and Jason into a false sense of security, because they were entirely unprepared the first time he unleashed a characteristic burst of ex-racing greyhound speed.

'The very first time we ever let him off the leash we were going to do some recall training. We took him to a little primary school with a fully fenced oval. We took him off the leash and he just took off,' she says. 'He went straight to the only part of the school that was not fenced and straight towards the main road. He had sprinted about six hundred metres by the time Jason was able to catch up with him.'

Magnus was deeply humble, but he did enjoy showing off his pace on the beach, too. 'People would stand back and say, "Look at that dog go." Other dogs would chase him and he would just kick it up a gear and say, "Nup." But he would always come back.'

With any other dog, the appearance of a sudden limp might not give particular cause for concern. Many breeds enjoy long walks and boisterous play, and a bit of roughhousing can cause the occasional bruise or tender muscle. But because 'layabout' was Magnus's default setting, and his rambunctious moments were so few and far between, Kristan was immediately worried when her beloved dog started limping one day in March 2017.

She tried not to catastrophise, but she knew that large breeds were more susceptible to bone cancer – known as osteosarcoma – than other dogs, and that greyhounds are the breed most commonly diagnosed with the condition. Though it can affect dogs of any age, it is more common in those older than seven; at nearly ten years old, Magnus was in the highest risk category.

Kristan took him to the vet, where he was prescribed a course of anti-inflammatory drugs. To her enormous relief, the limp disappeared completely and Magnus seemed absolutely fine.

As soon as he completed the course of medication, however, his lameness returned. That was when Kristan and Jason agreed to Magnus having X-rays and a bone biopsy.

Later that day, the vet called Kristan with the devastating diagnosis: Magnus had osteosarcoma in his shoulder.

'They called me at work and I cried so much they sent me home. We were just distraught. We thought, *This is our Magnus! Our perfect boy!* He was so healthy. We were expecting that he was going to live for at least another few years. We just wanted more time with him.'

There were options, but none could guarantee a long life. Amputation followed by chemotherapy offers the best life expectancy, but even with this drastic option, the average survival time is still only a year at most. Very rarely, a dog with osteosarcoma may live up to two years after diagnosis. With no treatment at all, dogs usually only have a matter of weeks.

Kristan and Jason, who married a year before Magnus's diagnosis, knew they couldn't put Magnus through amputation and gruelling treatment just to give him a few more months with a significantly reduced quality of life. Heartbreaking as it was, they elected not to treat him beyond managing his pain.

'We decided straight away that we just wanted to enjoy our time with him and to make him as comfortable as possible,' she says. 'Our thought process was, *We're going to give him an amazing life for as long as he has.*'

As they came to terms with a future they had never imagined, the couple spent a lot of time reflecting on what an extraordinary life Magnus had led already. He'd been a hard-to-beat racing dog and a lifesaving blood donor, and now he was a beach-loving senior couch potato whose 'parents' adored him.

Who knew how much more he could have achieved if not for this cruel diagnosis? What sort of adventures might he have had as he grew older?

Then Jason had an idea. Why should cancer curtail Magnus's adventures? As long as he was happy and well enough to get out and about, they didn't need to simply hide away and wait for the inevitable. There was nothing to stop him squeezing as many fun activities as possible into his remaining days and weeks.

Jason got out a pen and paper.

It was time to make a bucket list.

People have been compiling lists of things they want to do, see and achieve in their lives since time immemorial, but we have Morgan Freeman and Jack Nicholson to thank for the now ubiquitous term 'bucket list'.

The two screen legends starred in the 2007 buddy comedy *The Bucket List,* which is about two terminally ill men who decide to make a list of all the things they've ever wanted to do and then do them all in the time they have left – before they 'kick the bucket'.

Since the film's release, millions of us have compiled bucket lists of our own, whether or not we're dealing with a life-limiting illness. And plenty of us have made them for our pets, too.

Together, Jason and Kristan wrote down every possible experience or activity they could think of that would bring Magnus joy. It included things like swimming in the ocean, visiting an aged-care home, riding in a police car, meeting a celebrity and eating fish and chips on the beach (see the full list at the end of this chapter).

Then they set about figuring out how to make it happen.

'Initially we only shared the list with our family and friends on Facebook. "Who's got a friend that's a police officer?" "Do you have a boat that we can come on?" "Can we take him to the pub for a beer?"' says Kristan.

'The floodgates opened. People started piling in with offers to help us.'

The first offer they received was a cruise for Magnus on a stand-up paddleboard, so they did that the very next day. He also spent a day at school with Jason, where a colleague mentioned that his father lived in a nursing home. Did Magnus want to visit? Magnus did.

'He was so perfect. He took himself from room to room and to every chair. He was the right height, so the residents didn't even have to lean down to pat him,' Kristan says. 'He was amazing because he was so calm. That was him: always cool, calm and collected. Magnus was just unflappable.'

Word of Magnus and his bucket list soon spread. A journalist acquaintance of Kristan's wrote a story about him for the *West Australian* newspaper, accompanied by a short video. It soon racked up more than 60,000 views.

'Suddenly it was like the whole of Perth rallied together to help us finish the bucket list. I'd had a long day at work and I looked at my phone and it was just going off,' she says. 'Magnus's story really triggered something in people. It just really highlighted how much people love their animals.'

After the article was published, WA Police got in touch and offered to have Magnus tag along for a day. He enjoyed a ride in a patrol car and even a voyage on the Water Police boat.

Magnus felt the wind in his fur in the back of a vintage Mustang convertible, ordered treats from a gourmet dog-food truck, flew in a plane, ate sushi, and met not one but two celebrities: West Coast Eagles star Will Schofield and Hunters & Collectors frontman Mark Seymour.

He even got to be a big brother to some greyhound foster siblings, and Kristan says he was a great role model for them. 'He was so good at teaching them "how to dog". Sometimes the foster dogs would whip their heads around to look at him and see how he had reacted to something, and there would be no reaction so they'd think, *Oh, it's okay.*'

His favourite items on the list were any that involved food. 'He had his fish and chips on the beach. We bought him his own little portion, but he only wanted the fish. He's the only dog I've ever known who didn't like chips.'

The last item he checked off the list was meeting a war veteran. Kirstan says Magnus seemed to understand that something special was happening in those weeks, and that it was all because of him.

'He knew there was a bigger fuss than normal. I think he felt that this was the role he was born to play, and that this was his time to show that he was an absolute champion, a real celebrity.'

A happy by-product of Magnus's bucket list was that the media coverage increased awareness of two things Kristan and Jason had become passionate about: greyhound adoption and canine blood donation. 'We hoped to drum up a bit of interest about greyhounds and what wonderful pets they are.'

After 'two weeks of mayhem', the couple decided Magnus was ready for a rest. He had achieved every item on his list bar one – he didn't get to be a team mascot. But that was okay; Kristan, Jason and everybody who'd helped Magnus on his journey could see that he'd had a ball.

'I was always watching him for a sign that he was over it, but he never even came close to what I would have thought would be his threshold,' Kristan says. 'He'd had kids climbing all over him, pulling his ears, pulling his tail, but he never reacted. I think that was just how he was. He loved everybody.'

As much fun as completing Magnus's bucket list had been, some of the activities were a little bittersweet – none more so than his final play date with all his greyhound buddies. Magnus, Kristan and Jason had made many friends in the greyhound rescue community, and more than twenty-five dogs spent a glorious afternoon with Magnus in a pet-friendly café.

'One of the things I find most special about greyhounds is that they are so drawn to each other. When a greyhound sees another greyhound, it's like Christmas. They are so excited,' Kristan says.

'We were all crying at the end of the play date, because they knew it was the last time they would see him. We had all these experiences because of how fantastic he was, but there was always a little twinge of sadness behind all of it.'

Eight weeks after his cancer diagnosis, in April 2017, Kristan and Jason could see that Magnus's pain was too much for him to bear any longer. They made the sad decision to let him go. He was nine-and-a-half years old.

'We knew it was time to say goodbye. We had the vet come to our house and I'm so glad we did that. He was just at home with us and it was very peaceful.'

The couple was desolate without their beautiful boy, and imagined it would be a long time before they felt ready to open their hearts to another dog.

But just three weeks after Magnus died, they found they couldn't stand not having a four-legged presence in the house. 'The house felt so empty. We just hated it. So we thought, *Let's just get a foster dog.* There's always going to be a greyhound that needs a home,' says Kristan.

That dog, Lily, turned out to be a foster fail. 'It was love at first sight for Jason and Lily.' Kristan laughs. 'She pushed me to the side. *I'm here now, I've got this, I'm the lady of the house.* I missed my big, lovely boy, so I went out and brought home a male greyhound called Max.'

Tragically, Lily died from a severe bout of gastroenteritis in January 2019, but Max is now five and still thriving.

Kristan and Jason also added a two-legged member to their family: their son, Harrison, who was born in 2019. They had been trying for a baby while Magnus was alive and always felt sad that he didn't get to meet their little boy. So they gave Harrison a special middle name: Magnus.

'It's common for a family to name a child after a beloved family member and they don't get more beloved than Magnus,' Kristan says. 'He was so respectful and open to new experiences and meeting new people. He just moved gently through life. We'd love it if our son grows up to have some of those qualities.'

Kristan often thinks about how different her family's life might have been if they hadn't made the spontaneous decision to go and meet a homeless greyhound at a vet clinic on a searing summer day in 2013. What if they had talked themselves out of the idea because of their broken fence or their full-time jobs? What if they had adopted a different dog, or purchased a Labrador puppy instead?

Though she would have written a different ending to Magnus's story if given the chance, she doesn't regret a second she and Jason spent with him.

'We had decided that we wanted to give an older dog a second chance at life, and we got a dog that came into our lives needing so little from us but giving us so much in return,' says Kristan. 'There are some absolute gems out there. They just need someone to take a chance on them, and what they give back is exponential.'

The Norrises are now a 'greyhound family for life', and they have their young-old ex-racing dog to thank for it.

'We'll never have another dog quite like Magnus,' says Kristan. 'He was just something special.'

Magnus's bucket list

Go on a road trip
Have a professional photo shoot
Star in an ad campaign
Swim in the ocean
Foster another dog
Donate blood and save lives
Go for an ice cream
Fly in a plane
Try sushi
Eat fish and chips at the beach
Ride in a convertible
Order food at the drive-through
Go for a boat ride
Enjoy a gourmet meal
Meet a celebrity
Ride in a police car
Visit the elderly
Be a team mascot
Thank a war veteran
Compete in a dog show
Go to work with Mum and Dad
Go to the pub

Jonesy

The dog who was all ears

It could be said that a dog's longevity is a sign of a life well lived. Forget about strong genes and good health. Disregard simple dumb luck. Elderly dogs teach us that the secret to living happily to a ripe old age is choosing a person or people who will keep the treats, cuddles and good times coming.

After all, a pooch that keeps on keeping on well into his teens must have an existence worth sticking around for. And if that truly is the case, then Megan Grant's dogs have all lived the life of Riley.

Megan has always been an animal lover, and literally since day one she has shared her life with dogs. She was born among the rolling green hills of the Latrobe Valley, a part of the Gippsland region east of Melbourne. Megan and her family moved to the city when she was three months old, after her older brother, Tim, was diagnosed as being Deaf; Megan received the same diagnosis three months later.

'My parents decided to move us to Melbourne as they felt that my brother would have better access to specialist services being closer to the city,' she says. 'I was then diagnosed at six months old and fitted with my first hearing aids.'

Making the move to Melbourne with the Grants was Mindy the toy poodle. Later came Sam the Airedale terrier and Bunji the red heeler, who technically belonged to Tim, but was doted on by the whole family.

When she was seventeen, Megan fell in love with the first dog that would truly be hers. Leka was a basset hound–golden retriever cross, and looked every bit as unique as that mixture suggests. 'She was gorgeous. She had the body and bark of a basset hound, but the head shape of a golden retriever. My mum and I were living in Brunswick and she came to me via the local papers: Free to a good home,' Megan says.

'Like me, she was a water lover, and I remember that during our first walk she took herself off for a swim in a pond at our local park. Leka and I really gelled and I have lots of happy memories of her. She will always be very special to me.'

Leka was already three-and-a-half years old when she became Megan's four-legged best friend. When Leka was about five, Megan and her mum decided she could use a furry pal of her own. They adopted an eight-month-old blue heeler–Staffordshire bull terrier cross from the local RSPCA.

'His name was Apple and he'd had a tough start to life. He was very wary and found strangers very untrustworthy, but when Apple was with family he was very loyal and loving,' she says. 'He really bonded to Leka and he was a lovely dog.'

Leka was a stately nineteen years old when she passed away in 2010. Apple died in 2012 at the equally impressive age of sixteen.

Their unconditional friendship and loving presence was a comfort to Megan as she navigated the sometimes rocky terrain of growing up Deaf. She began her schooling at the Princess Elizabeth Junior School for the Deaf before switching to mainstream education at her local primary school when she was seven. She could speak and lip-read, and had lots of friends.

By the time she was a teenager, however, life was a little more challenging. 'I have many fond memories of my primary school years. But by the time I was in Year 10 I felt that I was being excluded from activities,' she says. 'Friends weren't asking me to the movies, and during conversations when I asked what people were talking about I would be told "it doesn't matter" or "it's not important".'

Megan decided to finish high school at the Victorian College for the Deaf (VCD), one of Australia's oldest schools for Deaf and hearing-impaired students.

'It was a move I do not regret. I grew up oral, but the college at that time was a signing school. It didn't take me long to learn Auslan, the sign language of the Australian

Deaf community, and I felt that I was able to fit in quickly,' she says. 'I felt that I was included and was not missing out.'

She didn't know it at the time, but moving to VCD would prove to be a momentous decision in more ways than one. It was there that she met her first hearing dog.

A hearing dog is a type of assistance dog that is trained to assist people who are deaf or hard of hearing by alerting their handler to important sounds, such as doorbells, smoke alarms, ringing telephones and alarm clocks. They have the same access rights as guide dogs for the blind and can go to every public place that people without dogs can go, with only a handful of exclusions, such as burns units in hospitals.

In Australia, hearing dogs are trained for and matched with their handlers by Australian Lions Hearing Dogs (ALHD), which was founded in 1980 by two Lions Club members from Adelaide. Lions Clubs Australia is a non-political service organisation that promotes medical research, disaster relief, and community, disability and youth services.

'I'd heard of hearing dogs, and when I was a student at VCD one of the staff there had a hearing dog named Bubbles,' says Megan. 'I didn't know of many other people who had hearing dogs, though.'

It would be almost fifteen years before Megan would start thinking about applying for a hearing dog of her own – but when she did, the perfect dog was ready and waiting.

If there's one thing Mary Knight knows, it's how to spot a good dog. All dogs are good dogs, of course, but for Mary's purposes some are good-er than others. Or rather, some simply have more aptitude for the tasks she wants them to perform.

Mary is a trainer and the puppy co-ordinator for ALHD. Each ALHD trainer is allocated up to four dogs at a time to train for their new Deaf or hard-of-hearing owner, with each dog at a different stage in its training.

In September 2006, Mary met a dog with the catchy name of VA861. That was the official identifier he'd been given at the Animal Welfare League of South Australia shelter, where he had been living for several weeks after being picked up as a stray. Somewhere along the way, though, shelter staff had nicknamed him Jonesy.

The handsome little dog was liberated from the shelter after eagle-eyed Mary recognised the traits of a potential hearing dog. 'As we walked past the different dog runs, he was right up the front of his pen, wanting to interact with us. He wasn't barking and appeared to be coping well in a stressful environment.'

Her interest well and truly piqued, Mary enquired with shelter staff about Jonesy's background. They didn't know anything about his former life, but estimated he was about three years old. As is common for dogs that arrive at shelters as strays, his age was an educated guess; Jonesy's 'birthday' was recorded as 5 September 2003 by the vet who desexed him on that date three years later.

Whatever had happened to him before he came to the shelter, it had helped to create a friendly and easygoing pooch. 'We took him into one of the exercise yards to do our assessment. This involves assessing his nature as well as his interest in sounds,' says Mary. 'Jonesy had a lovely nature and was not reactive walking past the other animals – he walked past other dogs and the cats.

'All hearing dogs are trained with the aid of treats, so it is very important that they are food motivated. Jonesy was very keen to receive treats from us, but he wanted to interact with us even before we offered him treats!'

At this stage, ALHD generally only selected dogs aged between six months and two years of age, but Jonesy was so impressive – and because smaller dogs like him tend to have a longer expected lifespan – he made the cut.

'We have only had a puppy program for the last two years, so before that it was only "teenage" dogs that came into the training program,' Mary explains.

So it was decided: Jonesy would become a hearing dog even though he was slightly older than other dogs in the program. He was assigned to Mary for training.

It takes six to eight months to train a hearing dog, during which time they live at ALHD's National Training Centre in the Adelaide Hills. By the time a hearing dog is delivered to its new owner, ALHD has spent about $37,000 on training them. However, the dogs are given to recipients at no cost as a gift from the Lions Clubs of Australia.

The training curriculum is divided into two distinct parts: the 'out training' and the 'sound training'.

Out training is designed to get dogs used to being out and about in a range of different environments. It includes things like trips into busy shopping centres and on public transport. They are also taught obedience, with those dogs that are going to a person who communicates with Auslan taught commands using hand signals only. 'Jonesy had to be on his best behaviour. He was also taken out for coffee to learn to lie under the table and not try to get food,' Mary explains.

Next came the sound training, which teaches the dogs to alert their owner to household sounds including oven and microwave timers, doorbells and knocks at the door, alarm clocks, incoming phone calls and text messages, and smoke alarms.

'All the training is done with treats, and starts with the dog being called to the sound, where there is a tasty treat waiting,' says Mary. 'The dog can also be trained to "go get" another person in the home if the handler needs help.'

Hearing dogs are taught to alert their owners by physical touch. Larger breeds sit and touch with one paw, while smaller dogs jump up and touch with both paws. After alerting, the dog then leads their owner to the sound and sits in front of it, ready for a reward.

Mary says hearing dogs adore their jobs. 'The dogs love their training as they get lots of attention and tasty treats, and have something to occupy their intelligent minds. It is more like a game to them.'

It may be a game for the dogs, but it's one that not only improves the independence and quality of life of their owner but can literally save their lives.

That was what was on Megan Grant's mind when, in 2007, she decided the time was right to find a new canine companion for herself – one that would help her to 'hear' the world around her.

Megan was about to celebrate a major milestone: her thirtieth birthday. She had a full and busy life that included a career in community services that she loved. Neither her Deafness nor her Usher syndrome – a genetic condition that means she is also legally blind – prevented Megan from travelling, socialising and enjoying all the independence of any other young woman living in one of Australia's busiest cities.

But Megan was plagued by a terrible fear that few people who don't live with sensory impairments ever have to contemplate. 'I was living on my own, and while I loved being independent, I was fearful at night-time about fire,' she says. 'I had frequent nightmares about my place catching fire, and bushfires. While there are smoke alarms available for people who are Deaf, I did not trust them.'

She didn't want to spend her life feeling afraid and struggling to sleep at night, so Megan contacted ALHD. 'I thought a hearing dog would be of benefit for me, especially alerting me to sounds I may not hear, or things I might not see, like flashing alerts or someone trying to get my attention.'

She applied for a hearing dog in late 2005 and settled in to wait for the perfect pooch. About a year later, ALHD got in touch to let her know she had been assigned a dog whose placement would be sponsored by the Lions Club of Carnegie: Jonesy.

'I was told that Jonesy was a fox terrier and that he could jump 1.8 metre-high fences,' Megan says. 'When a picture of Jonesy was mailed to me – this was before email became common – and I first saw him, I fell in love with him.'

Their first face-to-face meeting quickly followed. 'When I met him at the gates of my home, I could not believe how red his fur was. His colouring was technically tan and white, which is more what he was, but back when I first got him he was *red*.'

That was because Jonesy wasn't a fox terrier after all – at least, not entirely.

Because ALHD sources all of its dogs from pounds and shelters, there is no one breed that typifies the look of a hearing dog. Unlike guide dogs, which are usually Labradors or retrievers, most hearing dogs are crossbreeds. Over its history, ALHD has trained and placed more than 600 hearing dogs with Deaf and hard-of-hearing recipients, and they've ranged from working breeds like kelpies to Shih-tzus, Maltese and Chihuahuas.

There are currently about 100 active hearing dogs in Australia. Jonesy was hearing dog number 432, and was believed to be a mix of fox terrier and kelpie.

'I think that's about right. When Jonesy was alert, he had the pose and stature of a kelpie. He was basically almost like a miniature kelpie,' says Megan. 'Although when in the northern states, like Queensland and the Northern Territory, I had people asking me if he was part dingo!'

Jonesy officially moved in with Megan on 21 May 2007. If she had any worries about bonding with her new sidekick, she needn't have – their connection was instantaneous. 'Jonesy and I clicked right away. He was always eager to please, incredibly well behaved and very sensitive. And he *loved* alerting me to sounds,' she says. Just as Mary's training had intended, 'he thought it was a game'.

The only tiny teething problem Jonesy experienced was getting used to his feathered housemate, Megan's pet cockatiel, Eddie. She had already been a much-loved part of Megan's life for three years when Jonesy arrived, and they never quite managed to become friends.

'Jonesy was very wary of Eddie, but they tolerated each other,' says Megan. 'He'd get pretty sooky if she got too close to him, as he knew that if he tried to snap at Eddie he'd get in trouble.'

Perhaps a legacy of his mysterious former life, Jonesy revealed himself to be a sensitive soul. He very rarely put a foot wrong, but if he did make a mistake he was always terribly contrite. 'All I needed to do was say the word "naughty" and point my finger at him and he would get really upset, tuck his tail in between his legs and refuse to look at me. If he had an accident inside, like a little vomit, he would be really apologetic.'

While not a particularly playful pooch – a quirk shared by many assistance dogs – Jonesy did have a soft spot for one toy in particular. 'He only ever really played with one toy. He absolutely loved his green croc, and had several of them,' says Megan.

As the years passed, Megan and Jonesy adventured far and wide. Together they travelled to Broome, Cape Leveque,

Port Douglas, Townsville, Magnetic Island, Darwin, Kakadu, the Tiwi Islands, Hamilton Island, Sydney and Adelaide. 'We did many things together. Some of the best memories I have of us two are riding Horris the camel on Cable Beach and sailing the Whitsundays,' she says.

Jonesy was always 'on duty' when he and Megan were at home or on holiday together, but when they were out and about in public or at work at the Brotherhood of St Laurence, the not-for-profit where Megan is a local area coordinator, he was off the clock; there would simply be too many sounds for him to process. (He went to work with Megan anyway, because he was so devoted to her that he fretted when they were apart.)

Megan says Jonesy impacted her life in myriad positive ways over those thirteen years. His true value as both a best friend and an assistance dog is almost impossible to measure. One change that seems small, but is in fact quite remarkable, is that she now sleeps soundly.

'Since having Jonesy, my nightmares about fire have abated. I sleep better at night. Jonesy gave me the opportunity to be independent and I was able to rely on him,' she says.

And while officially he was Megan's ears, he also proved to be a huge help with her vision impairment. Usher syndrome means Megan can't drive, and she also experiences night blindness: her eyes take a long time to adjust to darkness, particularly when there is traffic and a sea of bright headlights. Walking after sunset was a treacherous endeavour before Jonesy came along.

'He was a great help to me at night. If I didn't have Jonesy, I'd normally end up tripping up the kerb onto the nature strip,' she says. 'I was always able to rely on Jonesy to ensure that I could safely cross the road. He made sure I crossed from one driveway to the driveway on the other side.'

Jonesy also appointed himself as Megan's in-house weather radar. Along with all his helpful practical skills, Jonesy came to Megan with an intense fear of thunderstorms, so he always made sure to let her know well in advance if there was one on the way. 'He was my thunder radar. I could always tell that a storm was coming twenty minutes before it hit us because Jonesy would be trembling,' she says. 'I could be sitting in a work meeting and announce that a storm was coming. My colleagues would ask how I knew this and I would tell them, "Because Jonesy told me so."'

Sadly, this ability slowly faded over time, because as he got older, just like his devoted owner, Jonesy became deaf.

Megan is no stranger to sharing her life with old dogs. After all, her childhood pets, Apple and Leka, lived to be sixteen and nineteen respectively.

But never in her wildest dreams did she imagine her faithful hearing dog would still be by her side after thirteen years. Astonishingly, when Jonesy passed away peacefully on 18 September 2020, he was at least seventeen years old – possibly even older, since his birthdate was a 'guesstimate'.

'I thought I would be incredibly lucky if Jonesy was still with me when he was twelve, but to still have him at seventeen was amazing,' she says. 'I have been lucky that all the dogs in my life have had long lives.'

Understandably, his advancing age affected Jonesy's role as Megan's hearing dog, largely because in the last years of his life he couldn't actually hear much at all. 'His hearing was just about gone. His depth perception changed, so he struggled with jumping up and down, steps, dealing with the change in colour contrasts, and coping with shadows,' she explains. 'He also became very slow physically. He was happy with just a walk around the block. Although in the afternoons, on our way home from work, Jonesy would go a million miles an hour, because he knew he was coming home to food!'

And after all those years of reassuring Megan at night, it was Jonesy who got jumpy when the sun went down. 'He was more unsettled in the evenings and would often be constantly pacing. Thankfully he slept very well.'

Despite the physical changes he had to adapt to, it was only in the last couple of years that Jonesy and Megan's relationship noticeably changed. She was diagnosed with breast cancer in July 2018, and it seemed to Megan that he aged very suddenly from that point. It was almost as if his mistress easing up the pace of her life was a signal to Jonesy that it was okay for him to rest, too.

'My diagnosis forced me to slow down, and I think this was when Jonesy aged quite significantly. Prior to my diagnosis his hearing was great, his eyes were fine. Physically he was quite good, just a little bit stiff,' says Megan. 'But during my active treatment Jonesy slowed down, and his age caught up to him. This was very obvious to me, because I was working to get back to full health but Jonesy was no longer able to keep up with me.'

Megan completed her active cancer treatment in April 2019, but will continue to take cancer prevention medication for several years.

Just as Jonesy worked to make Megan's life easier for so long, she was determined to do the same for him in his golden years. Twice a week, he would stay with his 'grandmother' – Megan's mum, Carol – and Megan used that time to squeeze in all the activities and outings she knew would be too much for her beloved little dog. 'I struggled to shop with Jonesy as he was too slow. So when he was at my mum's place I'd schedule all my appointments and do my shopping or go to pilates.'

He even had his own chariot, which enabled him to travel in comfort and style. 'He had a dog pram, which we used a lot on weekends. It's a nice twenty minute walk from my place to Mum's, but with Jonesy it took more than double that time, so the pram was very handy.'

Even with the adjustments she had made to both their lives, Megan knew that he couldn't continue as her hearing dog for much longer. In late 2019, she made the decision that it would be his last year as a working assistance dog. It was time for him to put his paws up and enjoy a well-earned rest.

Megan's employer was also aware that Jonesy would soon retire, but he was always a welcome presence in the office. 'They loved him so much,' she says.

Megan could never quite picture her life without Jonesy in it; she simply couldn't imagine a day when he wasn't by her side. After so long together, Jonesy wasn't just Megan's dog. He was so much more than a pet; more, even, than an assistance animal.

He was her best friend. Her right-hand man. A four-legged, tail-wagging extension of herself.

'I'd often think about life after Jonesy and how much I would miss him. He was a massive part of my life for more than thirteen years,' Megan says.

Having rarely been without a dog by her side throughout her life, she's sure she will have another hearing dog at some stage. 'I know that technology has advanced so much, especially with smart watches, and that will help my independence. But nothing will replace the role a hearing dog can play.'

But she will wait a little while before finding a new companion. Out of respect for Jonesy, but also because there are things she wants to do with the confidence and independence he has been so instrumental in building in her.

'I think I'll wait until I've done a trip overseas,' says Megan. 'I want to go to Greece and Croatia. I haven't been overseas since Jonesy came into my life, and it was only fair that I waited until he passed.'

Dogs as old as Jonesy arrive in shelters and pounds with heartbreaking frequency. It's as if, even after years of loyal companionship, their owners aren't willing or able to accommodate their changing needs. Even more sadly, some simply grow tired of their old friends and want a younger model.

It's a mindset that Megan simply can't wrap her brain around.

'What is an "elderly" dog? Dogs over the age of seven are seen as senior, but Jonesy was almost as active at fourteen as he was when he was seven. Why would anyone want to abandon or surrender their dog just because it's old and slow?' she says.

'Imagine if it was you. How would you feel if your family dumped you because you were too slow or had become too hard to look after? I believe every household should have a dog. They are a massive part of our lives and add character and love to a home.'

Indeed, if how deeply a dog loves and is loved in return were the key to a long life, Jonesy would have lived forever.

Tamana

The dog who loves life on two legs

Picture this: a world where animal welfare is truly taken seriously and animal cruelty has ended.

What would such a world look like? There would be no stray animals and no need for shelters or pounds. Pets would never be abandoned or abused. No animal would spend a moment of his or her life feeling hungry, cold or afraid; instead, every creature would know love and respect.

And every home would have a dog. Or a cat. Or several of both!

Sounds pretty great, doesn't it? That's the stated mission of World Animal Protection (WAP), formerly The World Society for the Protection of Animals, a not-for-profit international animal welfare organisation that has been in operation for more than three decades. Sadly, we're still a long way away from living in a perfectly pet-friendly world – and some countries are much further away than others.

WAP's Animal Protection Index (API) ranks fifty countries around the globe according to their legislation and policy commitments to protecting animals. Each country is awarded a grade, with A being the best and G the worst, reflecting how well that country looks after and advocates for its furred, feathered and finned inhabitants.

No country has yet been awarded an A, but the UK, Denmark, Sweden, Switzerland, Austria and the Netherlands have all earned Bs. Australia has a D grade, along with the USA, Canada, Russia, Turkey, Thailand, the Philippines and others.

At the bottom of the list is the only country to have incurred a G ranking: Iran.

The second largest country in the Middle East, Iran has some 83 million citizens, the vast majority of whom are Muslim. Religious beliefs may account for the lack of statutory protection for animals in Iran. While the Qur'an does permit the keeping of dogs for certain purposes, such as hunting and guarding, owning dogs as pets is considered haram – against the principles of Islam – because canines are believed to be unclean.

Despite this, in recent years dog ownership has become more popular in Iran, especially in wealthy neighbourhoods in the capital, Tehran. As a result, some hardline religious clerics consider dog ownership a sign of negative western influence. In 2010, Iran's Grand Ayatollah, Naser Makarem Shirazi, issued a fatwa – a religious decree – against keeping dogs as pets, claiming that 'many people in the West . . . love their dogs more than their wives and children'.

Iran also banned all ads for pets, pet shops, pet food and other pet products. The Grand Ayatollah added, 'Friendship with dogs is a blind imitation of the West.'

In 2014, conservative Iranian MPs passed a law that made it a crime to keep dogs as pets or walk them in public, with offenders subject to 60 lashes or a fine of up to A$3700, and the killing of the dog.

According to the API, Iran's government does not recognise animals as sentient beings, and has no animal protection legislation in place whatsoever. Animal cruelty is not prohibited, and there is no duty of care placed on pet owners, nor are there any regulations on the welfare of farm animals.

Unofficial statistics suggest there are about 2 million street dogs in Iran. The lucky ones are ignored, or perhaps even sporadically fed by caring residents. More commonly, however, stray dogs are abused and killed.

All of which is to say that it's tough to be a dog in Iran in general, and that life is particularly precarious for homeless dogs. Add disability into the mix and an Iranian street dog's chances of survival are slim to non-existent.

This was the grim reality facing a tiny spitz mix who was eking out a meagre existence on the streets of Tehran in the northern autumn of 2015.

Starving, filthy and terrified, the female dog's 'home' was an abandoned building. When she was found, she was paralysed, and judging by her injuries this was the result abuse. She could have died in that building and nobody would have known; she had no family to miss her.

But this dog did have *something*. A fighting spirit? Perhaps. An indomitable will to live? Maybe. Exceptionally good luck? Most definitely.

Because this broken, abused dog was found by people who cared – people willing to risk fines and public derision to save her life. They set the wheels in motion to bring this dog a miracle.

And, most importantly, they gave her a name – a name that means 'wish' or 'hope'.

Tamana.

There was never any doubt that fighting for the rights and welfare of animals would be a big part of Anya Todd's life. Growing up in rural Ohio, Anya has been an animal lover since day dot.

'I grew up with a flat-coated retriever, Ebbie, and always had cats, too,' she says. 'In middle school I became a vegetarian because of my love for my companion animals, and that decision really influenced me to get involved with rescue later in my life.'

In 2003, after living away from her small home town for several years, Anya returned and started volunteering at her local humane society. It wasn't long before she was asked to join the society's board of directors.

'By that point I had been involved in animal activism elsewhere, and as a vocal activist I didn't see eye to eye with the rest of the board on many issues. I thought we should be advocating for programs such as spaying and neutering, and ending the gassing of dogs at our local dog shelter,' Anya explains. 'Evidently the majority of board members did not agree with me and voted for my removal.'

But if being ousted from the board stung, Anya didn't let it get her down for long. Instead, she let it stoke the fire in her belly. In 2005 she established her own not-for-profit advocacy organisation, the Mid-Ohio Animal Welfare League (MAWL).

'Honestly, it was a good thing. I went on to form MAWL and eventually got the dog shelter to end the gassing of dogs, and assisted with a spaying and neutering program,' she says.

In the fifteen years since its founding, MAWL has continued to act tirelessly as a voice for the voiceless. It still provides low-cost desexing, as well as humane trapping of feral and stray cats, and community education programs.

The organisation also rehomes animals through its foster care service, removing dogs and cats from high-kill shelters and pounds, housing them with volunteers for as long as it takes for them to find permanent homes. When she set out that mission for MAWL, Anya couldn't have imagined how long that wait might be for one dog in particular.

In January 2016, Anya's friend Joy Smetzer, the founder and director of the Lasa Sanctuary for animals in Wooster, Ohio, told her about a dog in desperate need in Iran. Joy herself had rescued a dog through Tehran's MRT Sanctuary and brought him to Lasa – now she was determined to help other Iranian street dogs experience new lives in America.

This dog was called Tamana, and she was paralysed; x-rays had revealed she had a broken back and a bullet lodged in her abdomen.

'I hadn't rescued from overseas before, but when Joy shared the MRT Sanctuary's plea, I fell in love with Tamana's picture,' says Anya. 'I was told that it's not uncommon for dogs to be intentionally injured in that region of the world, and that the sanctuary had several paralysed dogs in their care.

'Being in rescue, I see pleas for help all the time, but Tamana's picture and story just struck a chord. And I knew we had an amazing group of supporters who would rally behind her.'

But getting Tamana to the United States would be no easy feat. Before Anya could even begin to wade through the paperwork and permits necessary to import a dog from the Middle East, she needed to find the perfect Ohio foster home for the plucky little pooch to go to when she arrived.

She decided to put the call out to her personal Facebook network before turning to MAWL's legion of supporters.

'If I can find a foster carer that I already know and trust, it's far easier in every way. If it's someone I don't know, the screening process does take some time – especially for a special-needs case like Tamana,' she says. 'I didn't want to waste any time. I knew she needed help ASAP.'

Anya also knew that Tamana's foster 'pawrent' would have to live in or near the city of Cleveland, which is home to the veterinary specialists MAWL uses. Most importantly, they would need buckets of patience and compassion for a dog that had multiple serious medical issues and would likely be scared beyond belief.

'I was looking for someone who would be home the majority of the day – Tam's paralysis meant she would need her bladder manually expressed several times per day – along with the fact that this was going to be a huge change for her,' says Anya. 'She was coming from a place with dozens of dogs, and she was travelling across the world. Tam would need plenty of time to decompress, so I was looking for someone who didn't already have a dog.'

The perfect someone turned out to be Janine Robb. She and Anya had become Facebook friends after meeting through the local vegan community. Just like Anya, as soon as Janine saw Tamana's picture online she was in love.

'I didn't really know Anya well; it was just by happenstance,' Janine recalls. 'Her Facebook post said, "I'm reaching out to friends first because I really want this dog to go to someone I know and trust."

'There was a video of Tamana. She was still able to stand for a few seconds if she had someone supporting her, and then she would topple over. Watching her struggle to even stand just tugged at my heartstrings and I thought, *I have to help her*.'

Janine ticked all the boxes in terms of what Anya was looking for in a foster carer. She frequently worked from home in her job in human resources, she was experienced with fostering pets with special needs, and she didn't have a dog.

In fact, Janine hadn't spent much time with dogs at all – she is most definitely a cat person.

'I grew up vegetarian and rescuing animals with my mum. We had a small farm and had rescue burros [donkeys], geese, chickens, ducks, llamas. We'd had a couple of dogs, but I didn't really know about dogs,' she says. 'I'm a big cat person. Even when I moved out on my own, I usually just had cats, and I fostered cats first. I had cats in and out of my home for years!'

But Janine knew she could provide a calm, loving home for Tamana for as long as she needed it, and she was up for the challenge of managing her paralysis and the associated medical issues.

So it was decided: Janine's suburban Cleveland home would be Tamana's first real residence. Anya told MRT Sanctuary she would bring Tamana to the US, and Janine excitedly began preparing to welcome her new furry foster friend.

'I got all the supplies and installed a doggy gate in my house. I got a crate and some blankets. I have a dining room area that has wooden floors, and I knew it would be the perfect spot for her to have her own space in the house,' says Janine.

Everything was ready. All that was left to do was wait.

Somehow the next two months seemed to both fly by and inch along at a glacial pace. With each passing day, Janine's anticipation and anxiety increased in equal measure.

'I was just waiting very anxiously. I was so nervous. I didn't know if I was going to be able to handle Tamana and take care of her properly. It was a roller-coaster,' she says. 'I had a senior cat at the time who had a lot of medical needs, but they were mostly related to old age. I didn't know much about Tammy. I didn't know what to expect – I just knew I had to help.'

Finally, in March 2016, Janine was at last able to stop wondering. After nearly two days of travel from Iran – in the company of another dog, Rocco, who had also been saved by MRT Sanctuary – Tamana landed on US soil.

'She and Rocco flew from Tehran to Germany and then to Toronto, each flight in the care of a human volunteer passenger that the Iranian rescue found,' says Anya. 'From Toronto, they were driven to Buffalo, New York, where I met them. When I first saw Tam I remember thinking how small she was in real life and how exhausted she must be.'

Tamana and Rocco parted ways in Erie, Pennsylvania – he went to another rescue, escorted by one of MRT Sanctuary's US representatives, while Tamana made the journey to Cleveland with Anya. The weary pair finally arrived at Janine's house at one o'clock in the morning.

Janine admits the wait for her new charge had been nerve-racking. 'The night she arrived, I was just a mess.' She laughs. 'I was so anxious and nervous, and she came here so late at night. It was crazy.'

Her first instinct was to smother Tamana – or Tammy, as she quickly became known – with love. But she knew the little dog would be overwhelmed. Instead, Janine set up

Tamana's travel crate in the dining-room area she had cordoned off for her. Then Janine waited some more.

But if she had expected reticence or even hostility, Janine was in for a delightful surprise.

'She came out of her crate and looked at me, and then she just came right next to me and snuggled into me a little bit. She kind of hid behind me,' she says. 'It was like she thought, *You look safe – I'll use you for protection*. I thought that was pretty amazing.'

Tammy was just as quick to make friends with Janine's cats. Well, two of the three cats.

'My two boys, Moose and Melvin, were fine with her within thirty minutes. They were like, *Okay, you're new, you're cool, whatever*,' says Janine. 'But I also have a girl, Q, and she did *not* like Tammy. She didn't want to be near this dog at all.'

(It took three months, during which Q lived entirely upstairs and refused to visit the ground floor at all, but eventually she accepted her canine housemate. 'She doesn't really interact with Tammy – she doesn't come up and say hi – but she's fine,' Janine says. 'It's funny, because she's Tammy's favourite cat. Probably because she never comes by!')

Next, Janine helped the brave dog to go outside and relieve herself. This brought another, more sobering surprise. While she had been prepared for the fact that Tamana might have bladder issues due to her paralysis, Janine hadn't realised until that moment that Tammy is actually physically unable to go to the bathroom without assistance.

'I knew she was going to have bladder issues and that I might have to express her urine, but she did pee on her own and I remember being really excited, like, *Oh my gosh, she can go on her own!* She's not strong enough to get it all out, though, so I need to squeeze to help her empty her bladder,' she says.

'But I'd never considered the other side – that she can't poop on her own. She tries, and sometimes it works, but most times it doesn't. Mostly it just comes out on its own when it's ready, often when she's sleeping.'

The curious thing was, Tamana's involuntary expulsions revealed something else about her. Her reaction when she awoke to discover she'd had a bowel movement in her sleep led Janine to suspect she'd had at least some basic training.

'She was definitely trained, which I wasn't expecting. When she first got here and was having accidents in the house I could tell she was ashamed that she did that,' she says. 'She knew it was bad, but she couldn't control it, so I wasn't going to yell at her.'

Could the abused and abandoned street dog have been a loved pet at some point? Tamana also understood some obedience commands, and Janine thinks she may have had a wider vocabulary in her native Farsi. 'I'm sure she knew some commands in Farsi, but she knew "sit" in English – I said it to her a few times and she just did it.'

Which isn't to say that Tamana's adjustment to her new life in America was all smooth sailing. She was understandably uncertain about her new environment, almost as if she didn't trust it. Nobody knew exactly how old Tammy was at that point – estimates ranged from one year old up to four – so it was anybody's guess how long she had been fending for herself, how many years she'd endured terrible abuse and suffering.

Given all she had been through, Tammy could be forgiven for expecting her safe, comfortable new existence to be snatched away at any moment.

'It took her a while to get acclimated to the house and the streets and the country. She was kind of just on edge,' says Janine. 'She never had an issue with me, though. She just took to me so easily. She's decided she likes me and I'm her person and she doesn't like anyone else.'

Indeed, Tamana was – and remains – slow to warm to new people. It takes multiple gentle introductions before she will accept an unfamiliar person, but Janine has devised an ingenious meet-and-greet scheme to help build Tammy's social skills.

'Meeting new people, we have to take it really slowly. Like, the first time you meet her, you can't touch her, and it can only be a few minutes at a time,' she explains. 'So I started having people come over just to socialise with her. Now there is a handful of people who can handle her and spend time with her. I have one friend who still comes over once a week and takes her hiking, so she has her hiking buddy.'

In fact, Tamana absolutely adores walking and hiking, which she does with the aid of a wheeled cart into which her paralysed hind legs are secured.

'Her favourite thing to do is hike, and it's amazing. Any time I'm getting ready to leave the house she starts dancing around and spinning in circles. I have some video of her hiking through the woods, through ravines, over rocks, over stumps, down steps – all in her cart,' Janine says. 'The longest she's done is 5 miles (8 kilometres) in one go. At the end of that I was limping and my hip was hurting and she was like, *Let's go!*'

As bold as she is in some areas, Tamana is fearful in others. She is frightened of loud and sudden noises such as fireworks, says Janine. 'She gets terrified. If I pop some bubble wrap, it scares the life out of her.'

As those first days of trial, error and new discoveries turned into weeks, and then months, Janine and Tamana's bond deepened. Janine knew she should try to maintain a little bit of 'foster carer detachment', but she couldn't help herself – Tammy was just too sweet.

'I was definitely in love with her. But because I've had experience fostering cats, I know the goal is to get them better, let them heal and then move them on so you can help the next one,' she says. 'I was very much on board with trying to get Tammy adopted.'

But that was the thing: Tamana didn't get adopted. Although MAWL regularly promoted her to its 3500-plus Facebook fans, nobody offered the courageous canine a forever home. Anya and Janine even set Tammy up with her own Facebook page – 'Tamana, the Paralyzed Dog' – and listed her on Petfinder, North America's largest database of adoptable pets.

Still nothing.

MAWL received plenty of enquiries about Tammy, but few of the people that asked for adoption forms ever filled them out. Those that did simply weren't the right fit for an ageing dog with a history of trauma and a long list of additional needs.

'She has come close, but people usually start backing away when I start telling them about the bathroom issues. When I say she poops in the house, I think it scares a lot of people away,' says Janine.

'One family who owned a pet shop wanted her. They were wanting to bring her into the store to be their mascot. I said, "I don't think that's going to work for her – that's not her personality." You can't not be watching her when she's around unfamiliar people. You have to be very careful with her.'

Her bathroom issues, which MAWL is always transparent about, also mean that Tammy is susceptible to urinary tract infections. Janine feels this is another mark against her in some people's eyes.

'She does have frequent UTIs because she can't fully empty her bladder, and because she poops when she's sleeping, she just tends to get bacteria back there. She has to get routine cultures and urinalysis tests, and she's on antibiotics a lot. It's not cheap.'

And there was another issue that undoubtedly put off some potential adopters. From the day she arrived, Janine and Anya had worked with a team of specialists to try to get Tammy walking on her own again. Many dogs with the type of injuries she has are eventually able to regain some mobility, so they were hopeful.

'The first eight months were the hardest with her, because we were fighting to get her mobile. She started going to hydrotherapy once a week, getting in the water and having the therapist "walking" her back legs for her. The therapist said that sometimes the nerves can reconnect and get that movement back,' Janine explains.

'Then at home I started doing the same movements with her, trying to activate the nerves and muscles. She saw a specialist in Columbus a couple of times to get leg braces fitted, and she did massage once a week.'

Eventually, however, all the people working tirelessly to get Tamana back on all four paws were forced to concede it wasn't going to happen. Not only was she not going to walk unaided ever again, her lifeless back legs were starting to decay. Everything, it seemed, was going against her.

There was only one remaining option to ensure Tammy could be as mobile and healthy as possible: amputation. But if nobody wanted her with four legs, would she ever find a home with just two?

Setbacks are a fact of life in the rescue world, especially when working with a dog that has as many challenges as Tammy. Learning she would not regain use of her back legs was a blow to Anya, but she didn't dwell on it. 'Of course, you always hope that walking will be possible, but she had already started to compensate fairly well by the time she made it to us,' she says. 'I knew she was resilient.'

Janine was similarly sanguine about Tamana's quality of life post amputation. She had seen what a burden the two useless limbs were for the happy-go-lucky dog.

'Her back feet were basically just dead limbs. They weren't getting enough blood circulation, so they were kind of rotting on her body. One foot was always raw and sore and bleeding,' she says. 'It started really bothering her.'

Nobody could say for certain how much sensation Tammy had in her hind end, but she worried constantly at her feet, to the point that she actually severed a toe.

'I kept wrapping them and putting antibiotic ointment on them, but they looked so bad,' says Janine. 'Finally the vet said, "It's just not working for her."'

And so, in November 2018, Tamana had surgery to amputate both rear paws, just below her knee joints.

Her recovery from the operation was slow and, it must be said, a little gory at times.

'I had to change her bandages three times a day because they kept sliding off. The wounds kept breaking open. At one point I could actually see her bones poking out,' Janine explains. 'After eight or nine months, she built enough scar tissue and it stayed closed.'

Despite the bumps in her road to recovery, Janine never doubted that the surgery was the right choice for Tamana. Nothing, it seems, can diminish her spirit, the love of life that seems to shine from her. Not abuse and neglect on the streets of Iran, not starting over in a foreign land, not repeated infections or phobias, not her advancing age, not paralysis, and certainly not amputation.

'She's way more mobile now because the legs were in her way and preventing her from moving comfortably. When she's in the house she's not in her cart, because she can walk and even stand fully upright on her stumps,' she explains.

Her stumps strap into her cart just as easily as her legs once did. 'Just seeing Tammy, especially when she's hiking, you can just look at her and know that she's so happy. She runs – I have to run to keep up with her! Her little ears bounce up and down. It's just awesome.'

Anya agrees that Tamana's approach to life is a lesson for us all.

'Knowing that she has been given so many opportunities that she didn't have in Iran has been the best part, from excellent medical care to knowing what a real home feels like,' she says. 'She has many people rooting for her, which is so lovely to see.'

Janine adds: 'I think she sees me and the handful of people who help me take to care of her as her protectors or her guides, that we're just here for her.'

Tammy has even become something of a poster girl for dogs dealing with paralysis or adjusting to life as an amputee. When Janine showed her vet video footage of Tamana racing along hiking trails in her cart, he was so impressed that he asked for permission to show it to other clients who were worried about their own pet's quality of life after amputation.

'She has no idea that she's handicapped. She's just like, *This is life*. I can tell she loves her life,' says Janine. 'People are always amazed and inspired by her.'

Which makes the fact that she's yet to find her forever home all the more perplexing. Rounding out her fifth year in foster care, it's believed Tammy is now somewhere around eight or nine years old, a senior citizen according to veterinary classification – though age has not slowed her down any more than the loss of her hind feet did. But despite regular enquiries, nobody has gone the distance after taking the initial steps to adopt her.

While Janine hasn't given up hope that the ideal family will someday whisk Tammy away, she's realistic about the brave dog's prospects. 'I'm on the fence. I guess I would be surprised if we found the perfect home for her now,' she says. 'Besides, I've had her for five years. Parting with her now would be a little more difficult. This might end up being a permanent foster situation!'

Anya is also hopeful that Tammy will be adopted, but for her there are other, equally important factors to consider.

'I am very surprised that Tam hasn't found a home yet. I thought her adorable face would have won someone over a long time ago, and I remain hopeful that she will find a home with people who will love and appreciate her,' she says. 'But I also hope that she continues to have adventures and happiness in her day-to-day life.'

That's what it comes down to for Anya, Janine, and everyone else who helped bring Tamana to the United States, and who has helped her since: she deserves happiness.

Even though she's a dog with a disability. Even though she's picky about who she trusts. Even though she's approaching old age.

If they had known back in 2016 that Tammy wouldn't walk again, that her ongoing care would be time-consuming and expensive, that she might never be adopted, would those involved in her rescue still do it?

Yes.

Without question.

Because Tamana is worth it.

'The throwaway mentality within our society is one of our greatest failings,' says Anya. 'Caring for senior and disabled companions can provide lessons in patience, hope, resilience, unwavering devotion, and the impermanence of life,' Anya says. 'I can't imagine my life without senior animals. All beings are worthy of love.'

Kato

The old dog who loves new tricks

It's probably the best-known canine aphorism in the book: you can't teach an old dog new tricks. This enduring adage, which is applied to humans just as often as dogs, would have us believe that growing old is a hardship – something to be tolerated rather than embraced. We're supposed to accept that 'maturing' means becoming cantankerous and set in our ways; that there is no adventure, learning, evolution or fun to be had once our hair (or fur) turns grey.

But Kato the white German shepherd seems to have missed the memo. Not only is he an old dog who *can* learn new tricks – and has a gaggle of state and national titles to prove it – he didn't hit his stride on that front until he was already a senior canine.

For Kato, as with so many dogs, ageing has been anything but a burden. Instead, it has allowed him to be the very best version of himself.

Kato belongs to Rachel Devenish-Meares, and he was always destined for a career in the sporting arena. A lifelong dog lover, it was Rachel's childhood experiences that made her vow to give her future canine companions lives filled with joyful thrills and healthy competition.

'I was that kid who pestered her parents for a dog for years. I got Sandy – the first dog that was really *mine* – when I was twelve. I'd always wanted a German shepherd, but my parents said, "We're not having a German shepherd – they're too big,"' Rachel recalls. 'Sandy was a weird cross of a boxer and a cattle dog, but we don't really know.'

Despite her not-being-a-German-shepherdness, Rachel adored Sandy. She was determined to have the best-behaved dog on the block, so she took her boisterous six-month-old pup to obedience classes in her hometown of Armidale, in northern New South Wales.

But this was the mid-nineties: training through positive reinforcement wasn't yet the norm. Punitive methods such as prong and choke/check collars were de rigueur. But even back then, it didn't feel right to young Rachel. 'I really didn't like it. We tried it for a while, and Sandy was very well behaved, but it just didn't sit right with me. I remember thinking, *The second I grow up and move out of home I'm getting a German shepherd and I'm going to train him positively.*'

In the meantime, she armed herself with knowledge. Rachel learned as much as she could about positive training practices, taking several courses and joining a local obedience club, where she taught classes.

Then, at the still tender age of twenty-one, she got Jaeger, whose name means 'hunter' in German. The handsome black-and-tan German Shepherd Dog (GSD) puppy was her first competition dog. He performed well in obedience trials thanks to Rachel's use of kinder training techniques, but she found she wasn't passionate about the sport. She knew the training made Jaeger a better canine citizen, but she didn't get a lot out of it herself. 'When I got Jaeger, I knew we were going to do competitions, and that I was going to train him to be the best I could, but even then it was like, "I'll do that because it's what I should do."'

Sadly, Jaeger's time in the obedience ring was short-lived. He was very young when he developed severe hip and elbow dysplasia, a hereditary skeletal condition to which large dog breeds are unfortunately prone.

He also developed debilitating joint conditions, and his reduced mobility and chronic pain meant Rachel was eventually forced to make the gut-wrenching decision to have her beloved dog put to sleep.

She was so devastated by his loss that she knew she would never have another black-and-tan GSD. 'He only made it to six, poor thing, and I was so heartbroken that I couldn't have another one like him. Even now, many years later, I struggle to look at black-and-tan shepherds and not see Jaeger and feel a bit heartbroken.'

But while her pain was too raw to open her home and her heart to another dog with Jaeger's colouring, Rachel was still hooked on the breed. There was no doubt in her mind that she was a GSD owner for life.

In the wonderful (and sometimes wacky) world of purebred dogs, the GSD is something of a Johnny-come-lately. Some dog breeds date back to 6000 BCE, but the GSD can be traced to 1899, when a German former cavalry officer, Max von Stephanitz, purchased a native sheepdog named Hektor at a dog show.

Von Stephanitz firmly believed that dogs should only be bred for working, and he had been looking for a canine that satisfied his requirements for the perfect working dog: strength, intelligence, alertness, loyalty, ability and beauty. Hektor apparently ticked all the boxes.

He changed the dog's name to Horand von Grafrath (you've got to love a dog with a surname) and declared him to be the first GSD. Horand was the first dog registered by the Verein fur Deutsche Schäferhunde (Society for German Shepherd Dogs), which Von Stephanitz founded, and is the genetic basis for modern GSDs.

The GSD's original job was to herd and protect sheep, but word of the breed's smarts and biddability soon spread. Today, these clever dogs are employed in a range of jobs including police and military roles, search and rescue, and disability assistance. And let's not forget performing: the famous canine movie star Rin Tin Tin was a GSD.

While the breed's most common colour palette remains black-and-tan or black-and-red, these days the GSD's thick double coat may also be sable, pure black, liver, silver or even a decidedly wolfish blue.

And then there's the colour variety that has captured Rachel's heart: pure snow white.

Once upon a time, white-coated GSDs were a big no-no. White dogs could not be registered with the society, and many white puppies were euthanised by breeders soon after birth. Over time, however, the white colouration grew in popularity, particularly in the United States and Canada, where a breed club specifically for white shepherds was established. (There is also the White Swiss Shepherd Dog, a variation of the GSD bred in Switzerland and recognised by the World Canine Organisation as a separate breed in 2003.)

It was partly this misfit status, as well as Rachel's emotional connection to the darker-coloured coats, that drew her to the white GSD. 'Back in the day, if a white puppy turned up in a German shepherd litter, they would put it down. It was considered a fault,' she says. 'The colouration is caused by a recessive gene; the white covers the other colours. It's the same thing that creates yellow Labradors, but for some reason the German shepherd people said, "No, we're not having it."'

Even after she got her first white GSD, the stunningly beautiful Schatzi, in 2003, Rachel often encountered shocking prejudice. 'People would say to my face, "I would have killed that thing at birth." I thought, *You can't discriminate against a perfectly healthy dog based on coat colour.*'

From the moment she saw her, Rachel felt Schatzi was destined to be hers. She was one of just two puppies remaining in the litter. Both were female and Rachel had long known she wanted a girl. There was also the fact that Schatzi was wearing a purple ribbon (breeders often tell their very young puppies apart by tying different coloured ribbons around their necks as makeshift collars) and Rachel, whose dogs always have a matching collar and leash, had already decided her next pooch would wear purple.

Even better, the little dog's original name was Treasure, and that was certainly what she felt like to Rachel (Schatzi is a German diminutive of 'treasure').

Rachel waited until Schatzi was about two years old before venturing onto the sports field with her. After her traumatic experience with Jaeger, she wanted to be certain the pup had finished growing and that it was safe for her to compete.

'Being bigger dogs, I like to make sure their joints are okay before we start jumping. I'm a little paranoid after Jaeger, because I did do some agility with him before I knew how bad his joints were. I thought, *I'm never doing that again*,' she explains.

But Schatzi proved to be a natural talent and an enthusiastic competitor at virtually every dog sport under the sun. In almost a decade of competition, the tenacious athlete earned seventeen titles in obedience, agility, sheep herding and Dances With Dogs (DWD), which involves dog and human performing choreographed routines to music.

Rachel's success with Schatzi, and more importantly the unbridled joy Schatzi displayed when competing, sparked a shift in Rachel's thinking. Dog sports and training were no longer things she did purely for the good of her pets – she saw they deepened the human–canine bond. They made her happy, too.

'I get so much enjoyment out of seeing the dogs have fun,' she says. 'It's that thing of seeing them work, doing what they're meant to do. Watching their minds work is just so fascinating.'

But Rachel is certainly no stage mum. In 2012, when she sensed Schatzi was losing some of her fervour for agility competition, she didn't hesitate to let her beloved companion retire. 'She gave up at nine and said, "Mum, I don't want to jump anymore." But she would come out and run through the tunnels and say hi to everyone and feel like she'd had a go.'

Schatzi could be forgiven for feeling a little weary by then. In January 2007, at the age of four, she had become mum to a litter of seven puppies, sired via artificial insemination by a white GSD in America. Six of the pups had already gone to loving homes, but Schatzi still had one of her offspring with her – and he was energetic, to put it mildly.

Rachel knew the instant she laid eyes on Kato that he wasn't going anywhere. 'From the moment Kato was born he was mine. It was one of those inexplicable things. I had them all marked with different coloured ribbons and he had the green one and I said, "Green boy's staying." Even at two weeks old I'd pick him up and he'd sit on my chest and I'd say, "He's the one."'

Kato was named after the character played by iconic martial artist Bruce Lee in the sixties superhero television series *The Green Hornet;* Rachel is a big martial arts fan. Kato's official kennel name, however, is Helter Skelter. It was a nod to one of Rachel's other passions: The Beatles.

It turned out to be a prescient moniker. 'I named all the puppies after Beatles albums, but I almost regret that because Kato really *was* helter skelter,' she laughs. 'He's always happy, smiling, singing his little songs. He just loves life. Every part of life is a joy to him. Even going for a car ride will make him sing for joy. He'll sit in the back of the van and chat to himself.'

Kato's joie de vivre was so irrepressible that he was a bit of a handful for much of his youth. He was particularly eager to join Schatzi in her various sporting activities.

'He kind of grew up on the sidelines, watching his mum do all the things. He would just be busting to get in there and have a go, even as a tiny puppy,' says Rachel. 'He even used to open the windows in my car to let himself out and come and join us at training. At the moment I have a van and I have to lock the sliding doors so he doesn't open them. He's smart – and he doesn't always use his smarts for good!'

Finally, in 2008, Kato was allowed to start training in agility. But if Rachel thought she had an unbeatable mother-and-son double act on her hands, she would soon be disappointed. Surprisingly, young Kato's relish for participation did not translate into success in competition that first year.

Or the second year.

Or the *third*.

Kato was a beautiful dog and a cherished family member, but when it came to canine sports he was just too rambunctious and easily distracted to meet the competitive milestones most dogs his age conquered with ease.

Was it possible he was a furry flop?

The situation was becoming embarrassing. It was 2015, and Kato was eight years old. At that age many top sporting dogs slow down a little, and maybe even start to think about retiring. The best of them have risen through the ranks by then anyway, conquering each competition level and earning the title that comes with it.

Not Kato. Though he was a senior dog, and his love of competing remained undiminished, he had yet to earn even a novice agility title. (Most dogs that compete regularly in agility earn theirs around the age of two.)

'He spent years in novice training, almost to the point of driving me to distraction,' Rachel says.

The problem was that Kato simply loved agility *too much*. He simply couldn't contain his passion for the pastime, which meant his performance at crucial moments could be a little, well, helter skelter. On the course, he well and truly marched to the beat of his own drum.

He didn't even start Dances With Dogs until he was six. 'It needs a measure of control that he just didn't have,' says Rachel. She went as far as taking him out of all competition for six months, hoping the break would help him mature and settle down a little.

It didn't work, serving only to further fuel the fire in his belly.

'He was too excited. He loved agility so much that he could not control himself.' Rachel laughs. 'He particularly loved tunnels. There would be a tunnel on the other side of the ring and Kato would look at me as if to say, *I'll be right back – I'm just going to go and do this tunnel!*'

By then, Kato had a younger sibling, Tora. She was then four years old and a relative newcomer to agility, but she was already nipping at his heels in competitive terms.

'At one point I was saying, "He hasn't even got his basic Jumping Dog agility title." I had someone ask me how old he was and when I said eight they said, "He won't do it now, then,"' says Rachel. 'I did have a little chat with him then. "Buddy, I need a little something here!" Tora was about to overtake him and it was like he went, *I'd better pull my socks up.*'

Eventually, Kato and Tora earned their novice titles on the same day in 2015. With his first taste of success in the ring, something seemed to click for Kato. It was as if all the pieces suddenly fell into place. 'He was technically a senior, but his brain finally chilled out a bit. He just went *bang, bang, bang* and started being successful. At the point when most people would be saying, "Okay, we're done," Kato was hitting his stride.'

Was he ever. In the six years after that first win, the elderly Kato earned a staggering twenty-eight state and national titles in agility, obedience, RallyO and DWD.

He took out the runner-up title in Queensland's 'Jumping Dog Excellent' category in 2018. At the 2019 DWD nationals, when he was twelve, he won the Intermediate Heelwork to Music and Freestyle Intermediate titles, then followed that up by winning the Queensland Intermediate Heelwork to Music category the very next day.

Rachel can't quite put her finger on precisely what changed in order for Kato to transform from enthusiastic wooden spooner to laser-focused winning machine. Her best guess is that he simply grew up enough to be able to master his wild and wacky impulses.

'He went from "cannot control myself" to being able to walk calmly in a straight line to winning at nationals. It was like he suddenly went, *Oh, you want me to* listen *to you!*' She laughs. 'I think he really hit his true peak at about eight, which is just ridiculous.'

Kato became one of those rare sporting dogs that are genuine all-rounders. Agility is his first love, but he's equally excited about obedience, DWD and Trick Dogs, which became an official dog sport in January 2020. (The only sport that Kato hasn't had much truck with is sheep herding, which Shatzi had excelled in, but that's because Rachel's club no longer has regular access to sheep.)

'You'll hear agility people say things like, "My dog hates obedience." Kato was never that dog. He doesn't care what we're doing, he just wants to be doing it,' Rachel says. 'He's never cared what the sport was as long as he was out with Mum.'

As to the magical quality that has allowed Kato to keep competing – and winning – well into his old age, that's a little easier for Rachel to define: it's joy, pure and simple. 'He just lives for sport. Any sort of competition, he lives for it. Of all my dogs, Kato in particular just loves it. You wouldn't think a dog could smile, but he smiles the whole time. He just absolutely adores it.'

And while she struggled to see much personal benefit in training and competition when she was a youngster, working with Sandy and Jaeger, Rachel says Kato's ability has increased her own happiness – not to mention her bond with her dogs – more than she ever thought possible.

'It's that feeling of when you have a really good run in a competition. You're so connected that you're like one being for that time: the dog is an extension of your body as you move around. It turned into not just being something for them; it's something for me as well,' she explains. 'They do get one-on-one "Mum attention" when they're running, and that's part of the thrill. I love seeing them enjoy things.

'I'm terrible about buying toys, because I love that look on their faces when you pull out a new thing and they're like, *woah!*'

Rachel, who in 2020 qualified as a canine fitness trainer and dog massage therapist, says people are frequently astonished when they learn that Kato is now an amazing thirteen years old. 'He's the oldest in competition by a long way. People who meet him often don't believe how old he is, because he just does not act like a thirteen-year-old dog. Even when he was hitting his stride at eight, people would come up to me and say, "How old is your puppy?"'

It was a long-running joke in Rachel's sporting community that it would be fitting for Kato to draw his final breath during an agility competition. 'All my training friends joke,

"Hopefully Kato dies midway over a jump, because you'll never be able to retire him,"' she says.

But even as the signs of ageing started to become more evident, she never really thought seriously about Kato's retirement. Why would she, when he was as energetic as he'd always been?

'He was starting to go deaf and a bit blind, but otherwise he was as healthy as an ox. The average lifespan for a German shepherd is twelve, so he was already past that. And he's always been a skinny little thing, because he never sits still!'

Rachel figured that whether or not Kato should retire wasn't her decision to make. Like Schatzi, he would let her know when he was ready to stop.

That was until, in February 2020, the decision made itself.

It started as a mild limp. One day it wasn't there and the next day it was.

'It was very sudden,' says Rachel. 'Kato was limping one day and I said, "Oh, that's not good." It didn't get any better, and having a bit of experience with joint and mobility issues, I was pretty sure it was an ACL injury.'

The ACL is the anterior cruciate ligament, one of the major ligaments inside the knee. In dogs it's called the cranial cruciate ligament (CCL), but it has essentially the same function as the human equivalent. In fact, a partial or full CCL rupture or tear is the most common orthopaedic injury in dogs. These injuries can happen all at once or gradually over many months or even years. A gradual rupture is the more common scenario.

Treating a torn CCL usually involves surgery, though conservative management – such as a knee brace to stabilise the joint, or supplements that support joint health – is also an option.

Rachel took Kato straight to the vet, where his partial CCL rupture was confirmed. 'It's not completely torn, but if he does anything like jumping it *will* completely tear, and at his age it's hard to fix things,' she says. She knew his sporting career was over. She simply isn't prepared to risk her elderly companion being forced to have invasive surgery.

So just like that, Kato retired from agility, RallyO and DWD. He still competes in Trick Dog, because Rachel is able to choose low-risk tricks for him to perform. And also because, 'I think he would go insane if he didn't have something to do.'

Many thirteen-year-old dogs would welcome the opportunity to put their paws up, but not Kato. It has been hard for him to adjust to his suddenly sport-free world.

'It's hard because his brain tells him he's still a two-year-old. He'd try to do it on three legs if given the chance,' Rachel says. 'It's tough for him, but I think to some extent he understands, *It will hurt if I do this*. I've just got to find other ways to keep that brain active, because he still has so much desire to do things.'

Compounding the injustice is the fact that Kato has to watch from the sidelines while sister Tora and brother

Dojo, a two-year-old white Swiss shepherd, continue to compete. Schatzi passed away in 2018 at the age of fourteen.

Rachel knows he's longing to be out there with them, and for her that's the part that hits her right in the heart. 'I had the others at an agility competition and every time I moved, Kato would give me these big eyes like, *Is it my turn?* At training I let him go out and run through the tunnels, just so he can feel like he's had a go,' she says.

'We're lucky that Trick Dogs has come in as a new sport, because I can tailor that to things that aren't going to hurt him. I have to keep doing things for him, training wise, that he can handle.'

While some dog owners might consider it a burden, for Rachel it's a privilege to be able to create and discover new ways for her four-legged friend to wring maximum enjoyment out of life.

Old dogs are a gift, she says. 'Kato is just as cute now as he was when he was born. The eyes are a bit cloudy and the face goes a bit grey, but there's just as much love in that face as there was when he was tiny and fuzzy.'

There's the small matter of balancing the books, too. 'Old age is the time where you give back to them. He's given me everything he has, all his joy, for thirteen years. Now is the time when I repay that. It's up to me to give him the best end of his life,' she says. 'He's perfectly happy to lie at my feet and just be. Every now and then he'll pop his head around the corner, give me a smile and walk off, as if to say, *Hi Mum, I'm still here and still happy.*'

And there are also advantages to living with a dog who's finally outgrown his helter-skelter habits: 'At least he's not breaking out of cars like he used to!' Rachel laughs.

Kato may never win another title or even participate in another competition, but he has undoubtedly lived life to the full. And with his unfettered delight at being alive, his hunger for fun and endless capacity for play, Kato has been the ultimate role model for a good life.

'My mantra in life is, "Be like Kato." He sees the joy in the little things, the simplest things in life, like, *I got to tackle that jump and it was awesome!* Just going in the car to go to training is exciting to him,' she says.

'Just find the fun and enjoy the fact that you're out there with your dog, and the rest doesn't matter.'

Be like Kato, indeed.

More Information

Arnie
janecanfield.com
Instagram: @janecanfieldartist

Chaser
chaserthebc.com
Instagram: @chaserthebordercollie

Chilli
vickiaustin.com.au

Haole
awalkonwater.org
Instagram: @haoleboysurfs

Jonesy
lionshearingdogs.com.au
Instagram: @aus_lions_hearing_dogs

Maya

facebook.com/DetectionDogsForConservation

Suzy

Instagram: @suzynpupman

Tamana

facebook.com/TamanaParalyzedDog
facebook.com/midohioawl

Acknowledgements

First and foremost, my heartfelt thanks to each and every one of the wonderful dog owners who shared their pets' remarkable stories with me for this book. My interviews with each of you were a mix of joy and laughter, and in some cases tears and sorrow, and getting to know you all has been my absolute privilege and pleasure.

Extra hugs to Kim and John Murphy, Megan Grant, and Karen James, whose adored canine companions Haole, Jonesy and Puppy passed away during the writing process, and to Vicki Austin, whose best mate Chilli received a life-limiting diagnosis shortly after our interview. You all gave your dogs the best, most fun-filled lives, and they absolutely knew how much they were loved. I truly appreciate your willingness to continue even as you were grieving for your four-legged friends.

Thank you to the best editors a gal could ask for,

Johannes Jakob and Alison Urquhart at Penguin Random House. Your editorial guidance (not to mention your cheerful willingness to accommodate my various deadline-pushing catastrophes) is so important to me. Thanks also to designer James Rendall for creating this book's beautiful cover.

Much of Australia was on fire as I wrote this book during the summer and early autumn of 2020, and I was delighted to be able to support Victoria's Country Fire Authority (CFA) via the #authorsforfireys Twitter auction organised by YA authors Emily Gale and Nova Weetman. The wonderful Annemieke Jongsma and her adorable rescued Amstaff-Bordeaux mix, Odin, were the winning bidders of a special acknowledgement in *Extraordinary Old Dogs*. Annemieke, thank you so much for your generous bid, for reading all my books, and for being such a devoted dog mum to Odin. He has the life he deserves thanks to you. Happy reading, and keep loving dogs!

All my love and gratitude to my family, especially my husband, Mark, our daughter, and our three ridiculous dogs. Thanks to the friends that buy my books and say nice things about them, and especially those who facilitate the writing by entertaining my child for hours at a time. Cheers also to the media, bookshop staff and librarians that promote my books, host events, and invite me on their shows to gush about dogs.

Thanks to the team at my local community radio station, Radio Blue Mountains, for supporting my weekly pet show, Pet 'N' Wild. It airs Wednesdays at 5 p.m. AEST on 89.1FM in the mountains, and online at rbm.org.au. Don't miss it!

Finally, thanks to my sweet old puppy man, Tex. I hope he's still hanging in there when this book comes out so that I can annoy him by insisting he have his picture taken with it.

Discover a
new favourite